TRACTOR PULL!

Scott Webb

MBI

First published in 2004 by MBI, an imprint of MBI Publishing Company, Galtier Plaza, Suite 200, 380 Jackson Street, St. Paul, MN 55101-3885 USA

MBI titles are also available at discounts in bulk quantity for industrial or sales-promotional use. For details write to Special Sales Manager at Motorbooks International Wholesalers & Distributors, Galtier Plaza, Suite 200, 380 Jackson Street, St. Paul, MN 55101-3885 USA.

ISBN 0-7603-2001-2

On the front cover: Darren Smith of Crittenden, Kentucky, on 8,200-pound Super Stock *Walking Tall* at the 2003 Louisville Championship Tractor Pull. *Photo Joe Egli*

On the frontis: Lance Little of Tuscola, Illinois, getting the most out of *Gang Green* at the Monroe County Fairgrounds, Monroe, Michigan. Little's John Deere 6030 Prostock tractor ground to a halt after 267 feet. *Photo Joe Egli*

On the title page: Joe Eder driving one of his championship rigs— *The Odd Couple.* The charismatic Eder, of North Collins, New York, added to his impressive trophy case in 2004 with a win in the 7,500-pound Modified class at the Louisville Championship Tractor Pull. *Photo Joe Egli*

On the back cover: [1] Dave Snyder of Hudsonville, Michigan, with his modified tractor, *Space Invader,* powered by two GE T-64 Gas Turbines, each with a shaft horsepower of 4,330 and a turbine inlet temperature of 1,520 degrees. [2] The *Silver Bullet* is the alcohol-burning, Caterpillar-3208-powered, AGCO-White Super Stock rig of Jordan Lustik of Eighty-Four, Pennsylvania.[3] Bernie Platz of Sigel, Illinois, on the A-C Superstock tractor *Lil Bad Allis.*

AUTHOR BIO: Scott Webb has been an engineer, and has worked as an editor and writer in the agriculture and construction equipment industry for nearly a decade. He was a major contributor to *The Caterpillar Century,* a historical retrospective on Caterpillar's equipment milestones. He resides in Madison, WI.

ACKNOWLEDGMENTS: A complete history of tractor pulling would be the work of a lifetime and would take many volumes. This book highlights pullers who have reached the highest levels of consistent success in National Tractor Pullers Association (NTPA) or American Tractor Pullers Association (ATPA) pulling. It could not have been written without the gracious assistance, in terms of both information and photography, of Gregg Randall and the WPI/NTPA, Tom McConnell and the ATPA, and Photo Joe Egli.

Edited by Steve Gansen and Lindsay Hitch
Designed by Rochelle Schultz

Printed in China

Contents

Preface   6

Introduction   8

CHAPTER 1   The Roots of American Tractor Pulling   11

CHAPTER 2   The 1970s—Multi-Staging   21

CHAPTER 3   The 1980s—Classic Confrontations   37

CHAPTER 4   The 1990s—Shifting Gears   51

CHAPTER 5   Pulling in the New Millennium   77

Index   94

Preface

The sun is dropping low among the spokes of the Ferris wheel behind the grandstand, and for the first time, standing at the edge of the track, you smell it—a mixture of funnel cakes, diesel fuel, and the giddy expectation of a waiting crowd.

It whispers to you—something about glory, something about anticipation—from a place close to your heart, but even closer to your gut. It talks about things you feel, rather than things you know, like the shattering roar of a Modified pulling tractor coming off the line. Images flash through your head—spinning wheels, flying dirt, a front end slowly nodding up off the ground as if to say, "All right, you asked for it. . . ."

The first hook is up. Like a chained beast, it trembles, waiting for a signal to charge. Suddenly, somewhere deep in its metal heart, liquid squirts down a row of cylinders and the rapid-fire explosions well up from the earth beneath your feet.

Inside the cab, a clutch pedal rises. Bits of track fly skyward as tire lugs search the auburn clay for a foothold, and find it. And in that moment, as the sled lunges off the mark, you remember why you came.

Introduction

There is no motor sport that compares with tractor pulling. While cars dispute the issue of speed over a quarter-mile or hundreds of miles, nothing approaches the test of brute force that a modern tractor pull provides. It's different, and for fans of pulling, that difference is an addiction.

From the beginning, the sport had a calling all its own. Tractors are not like other wheeled machines—they don't just move people around, they work for a living. And that difference carries over into the sport.

The winner at Daytona will travel 500 miles and hit 200 miles per hour on the straightaway. A top fuel dragster can clear 300 miles per hour and cover a quarter-mile in under 4.5 seconds, as the driver pulls up to 8 gs.

Tractor jockeys don't pull gs, just the sled. This sport values strength, and that feeling goes beyond the track into the lines of waiting competitors, and on into the grandstand.

The people of pulling are just like tractors— tough, built to last, and there when you need them.

Even when tractor pulling started to include trucks, it stayed true to its basic values—strength, family, and sportsmanship.

And while the speed motor sports evolved into global media events—flashy and exciting in their own right—tractor pulling has found its own path as the sport of pure power.

Of course, there's more to it than just power. You've got to be able to find enough friction underfoot to get all those horses to actually pull something and not just spin around in circles.

And that's where experience counts, where commitment begins to pay off.

And it is commitment, both professional and personal, that has made tractor pulling what it is today.

Nobody has gotten rich pulling a sled. There are very few Rockefellers in the stands. Tractor pulling was not built with the investment of millionaires, but with the simple caring efforts of people who love the sport—either watching it, or competing in it.

It began with the simple desire of neighbors to get together for some backslapping and friendly competition.

Some people liked tractor pulling for the effect it had on their families. For others, the tractor pull was simply where their friends were. Some just liked the sound of it—the *feel* of it.

And slowly, it grew. The gatherings became larger. The tractors became stronger. Competition became keener.

In 1969 the National Tractor Pullers Association (NTPA) started to organize competition and lay out a few ground rules. Heroes began to emerge—the Banter brothers, Danny Dean, Bruce Hutcherson, Esdon Lehn, Tim Engler.

More associations sprang up. More divisions of pulling competition emerged. What had started with two kinds of tractors—stock or definitely not stock—became an event where almost anything that could pull a sled would be tested.

Pickup trucks, semi trucks, tractors burning alcohol, tractors with airplane engines strapped to the chassis, they all hooked up and gave every ounce of horsepower they had to the sled.

New, younger heroes replaced the older ones, some of them the sons of great pullers—Scott Smith, Craig Nation, Larry Shope, Tom and Rodney Martin, Greg Hibbitts, and many others.

Even younger ones, whose names we do not yet know, wait along the track for their first hook.

And the sport continues to grow, for the same reasons it started—a little backslapping amid the thunder; a gathering of friends and family; the feel of a tractor digging in.

These things, like diesel to a smoker, will fuel a new pulling century.

CHAPTER 1

The year 2003 was a great one for Joe Eder and *Odd Couple* of North Collins, New York—he won the Grand National Championship in the Modified division after surrendering a 12-point lead to Doug Downs' *Predator*. After a poor start in Tomah, Wisconsin, Eder won 17 out of 19 hooks. *Don Gillespie*

The Roots of American Tractor Pulling

No one can say exactly when people began to gather and test the strength of their early farm tractors. In the 1800s and early 1900s, horses in farming areas were matched in a crude version of the modern tractor pull. Long before television and modern entertainment, these back-forty gatherings were a much-anticipated chance to gather, settle the issue of who had the highest horsepower, and maybe even come away with a dollar or two from a well-placed wager. As plow horses gave way to 25- and 30-horsepower tractors from the Holt and Best companies, and then from the Caterpillar Tractor Co., these competitions grew in size and excitement.

The first attempt at organization came in 1929, when the first documented piston-engine tractor pulls were held in Vaughnsville, Ohio, and Bowling Green, Missouri. These were simple, dead weight pulls, the sledge pan loaded with whatever was heavy and available. As larger contests evolved, they remained crude dragging matches. Sledges and pans were loaded with whatever lay within reach, even other tractors. The pulling machines themselves, of course, were stock tractors. They might be stripped for the event, but there was generally little contest preparation, if any.

Dead weight pulling had disadvantages, however. Once the boulders and feedbags and piles of manure got going on the sledge, distance was no longer an object. So the real test was to find the amount of weight that only one tractor could move—a tricky and sometimes lengthy process.

These early pullers came up with a simple, sensible solution—the step-on sledge. To meet the need for an increasing load, eager participants would simply hop onto the sledge in regular intervals as it passed by. When the puller ground to a halt, the distance was measured, and everybody went back into position for the next pull. It was a good way to get fans involved in the pull, but it lacked precision. People wandered off for various reasons and had to be replaced, always by someone a bit stouter or thinner, thereby casting doubt on the results and leading to squabbles.

Post-pull fights notwithstanding, the step-on sledge made for a much faster and more entertaining pull. The sport began to catch on. These were glorious days for pulling, when anyone could scrape together a few bucks, get a broken-down International Harvester and an old Chevy, take the engine out of one and put it in the other, and head off to the county fair.

TRANSFERRING WEIGHT

By the 1960s, pullers were fitting turbochargers to stock engines or dropping V-8s into factory chassis and parading their machines on the fairgrounds of Columbus, Ohio, and Milwaukee, Wisconsin, for popular events. People still hopped on the sledge as it ground by, but now it took a lot more of them to bring the machine to a stop. The sledge was becoming crowded, and until a 6-miles-per-hour speed limit was imposed, it was no place for the slow-of-foot.

Despite the hayride appeal of the step-on sledge, as the prize purses grew larger, the inaccuracy of the system became more glaring. If a friend was pulling, a man was likely to stand on the very back edge of the sledge to ease friction. A less popular puller might find everyone crowded forward trying to get the sled to dig into the track. The sport needed a more objective, scientific measure of pulling power. Enter the weight-transfer sledge.

The weight-transfer sledge was truly an invention of genius. It did the same job as the old jump-on sled—increasing resistance to a pulling tractor—without adding any weight! Instead of adding more weight along the track, the weight-transfer sledge merely shifted weight from rolling wheels aft to a large steel plate in front. The overall weight of the sled remained the same, but the tractor started out pulling that weight in a wagon, and ended up dragging it like a bathtub. The weight-transfer sled was basically a semi trailer flatbed that rested on wheels in the rear

Bill Leischner, ATPA Grand American Champion in the Super Modified class, is shown here in his 2WD Ford truck known by the same name as his Modified winner, *Dirt Slinger.* Leischner is from Weldon, Illinois. In the ATPA Winternationals on January 18, 2004, *Dirt Slinger* came in seventh place in the Super Modified 2WD Trucks division behind winner Stan Shelton in his Ford *Cutting Edge. Don Gillespie*

Bob Jostock of Lapeer, Michigan, 1996 Grand National Champion, has a little engine trouble. Jostock's 7,500-pound Modified Tractor, *Wild Child*, is shown here at the Louisville Championship Tractor Pull on Saturday, February 15, 2003. A year later Jostock placed fifth at Louisville behind winner Joe Eder. *Kentucky Fair & Exposition Center*

13

Anybody who has ever gotten down on all fours to blow on a campfire knows that it burns a lot hotter and faster with more air. Not long after automotive engines were invented, engineers discovered that the same principle holds for internal combustion.

Blowers and Turbos

When the homegrown engineers of tractor pulling started looking to make their cylinder fires hotter, getting more air into the combustion chamber was one of the first things they tried. Adding a turbocharger or supercharger is one of the best and easiest ways to pump up an engine's horsepower without significantly increasing its weight.

These devices compress the air flowing into the engine, squeezing it down into the combustion chamber of each cylinder. Of course, then you add more fuel. More air, more fuel, more boom.

And more boom means more horsepower.

The main difference between a turbocharger and a supercharger is the power source. A supercharger uses a belt running off the engine as its power supply, while a turbocharger is driven by exhaust gases already produced by the engine.

A turbocharger's design rpm is typically extremely high—perhaps between 10,000 and 15,000 rpm at low engine speed and up to 60,000 to 100,000 rpm at full engine speed. At 1,667 full revolutions every second, that thing's really hummin'. And since it's hooked up to the exhaust, the temperatures in the turbine tend to be quite warm. With warm parts longing to fly away from the spinning hub, there is a potential for danger. To be safe, most regulations state that the turbocharger has to be shrouded.

There are tradeoffs in both systems. In theory, a turbocharger is more efficient because it uses the "wasted" energy in the exhaust stream for its power source. On the other hand, a turbocharger causes some amount of back pressure in the exhaust system and tends to provide less boost until the engine is running at higher rpm. Superchargers tend to be easier to install, but more expensive.

Turbos and blowers are only allowed in certain classes of pulling, although rules can vary. Modified minis and 4WDs have to be naturally aspirated, according to National Tractor Pullers Association (NTPA) rules, but pressure stages are allowed in the 2WD, Modified, Semi Truck, Super Farm, Prostock, and Super Stock tractor classes.

Super Stocks are allowed up to four turbochargers, all connected together, which is quite a feat of engineering. Each stage crushes the air coming into the engine into a smaller and smaller space. At the end of the last stage, static air pressure can reach 200 psi, over 13 times normal air pressure at sea level.

Check out the turbocharger on Jordan Lustik's *Silver Bullet*. The *Silver Bullet*, an AGCO-White 6195, is powered by an eight-cylinder 3208 CAT engine. This power plant is a powerful mover in its basic, stock form. The Lustiks' modifications improved its horsepower rating dramatically, from a maximum of 270 toward the 3,000 horsepower mark. *Don Gillespie*

of weight transfer, and therefore resistance. Over the years, tractors grew more and more powerful, and this resistance control became a helpful feature.

GETTING ORGANIZED

By 1969, with record crowds attending pulls all across the Midwest, there was no doubt that this informal, individualistic sport was here to stay. The time had come for some organization. A few rules were needed, as well as planning and promotion. With that in mind, representatives from Minnesota, Missouri, Iowa, Indiana, Illinois, Pennsylvania, Ohio, and

Richard Bonner of Mantua, Ohio, pulls an Ironman sled in *Unforgiven,* a John Deere 10,200-pound Prostock Tractor, at the Louisville Championship Tractor Pull in 2003. In 2004, Bonner and *Unforgiven* placed seventh in the preliminary round of the Prostock Tractor division with a pull of 219 feet. *Kentucky Fair & Exposition Center*

and a steel plate, or pan, in front. It was then fitted with a large weighted box on rails running fore and aft.

In operation, a mechanism driven by the turning wheels moved the box toward the front of the sled. With every revolution of the wheels, the heavy box shifted more weight from the wheels onto the pan, making it harder and harder to pull. The tractor either made it the full 300 feet, or quit along the way, and the pull was measured. A number of advances on the basic concept followed—sleds eventually became motorized so they were handier to maneuver; different transmission ratios gave operators more control of the rate

A couple of great pulling fans show their allegiance on their jackets. Few sports can match the family involvement of tractor pulling. *Don Gillespie*

Michigan agreed to form the National Tractor Pullers Association (NTPA). On April 12, 1969, the NTPA held its first meeting in Ottawa, Illinois. The NTPA established two divisions of pulling, Stock and Modified, and within each division weight classes matched tractor size for fair competition.

That same year, a group of pullers started the Championship Tractor Pull at the National Farm Machinery Show in Louisville, Kentucky. With the double draw of a world-class farm equipment trade show and a world-class tractor pull, this invitation-only event grew to become the premiere indoor tractor pull, eagerly anticipated throughout the year. A year later, for the first time, the NTPA established a championship in its pulling divisions. Through a circuit of pulling events during the season, points were awarded based on place of finish. At the end of the season, points were tallied and a winner announced.

Joe Kwiatkowski of Dorr, Michigan, won the 8,000-pound Super Stock Alcohol division of the 2002 Louisville Championship Tractor Pull. Kwiatkowski also won the NTPA Grand National Championship in the Super Stock Open division in 2001 and 2002. He is shown here in his John Deere 9200, *Taking Care of Business. Don Gillespie*

Jordan Lustik from Eighty Four, Pennsylvania, is one of the most successful and popular stars in modern pulling. His alcohol-driven Super Stock tractor, *Silver Bullet*, won the 2002 ATPA Grand American Championship, among other titles. *Don Gillespie*

David Batliner of Floyd Knobs, Indiana, runs his smoking Massey-Ferguson 8160 *Superhick* at the Louisville Championship Tractor Pull. Batliner finished 11th in the preliminary round of the Louisville show in 2004 in the 9,300-pound Super Farm Tractors division behind Larry Wolff in *Wolffgang's Warrior. Kentucky Fair & Exposition Center*

Butch Krieger, veteran pulling announcer, stands with his boys. Krieger has been the announcer of the Louisville event for 25 years. For many fans, Krieger is the voice of the Championship Tractor Pull. *Don Gillespie*

CHAPTER 2

Dave Banter drove a single-engine Modified tractor back in the days when a man went pulling bareheaded in a white T-shirt. This rare photo depicts the beautiful simplicity of the older Modified tractors. *NTPA*

The 1970s—
Multi-Staging

At the beginning of the 1970s, there were no safety requirements for machines, mechanics, or fans. With horsepower climbing steeply, and pullers experimenting energetically with no oversight, accidents were almost assured.

Moving to avoid catastrophe, in 1971 the NTPA executive board required all automotive V-8s used in tractor pulls to be equipped with bell housings, flywheels, clutches, and automatic transmissions approved by the Special Equipment Market Association (SEMA).

In the Modified division, horsepower-hungry pullers were sizing up an engine used in World War II fighter aircraft. It was a 1,710-ci, 2,000-horsepower V-12 built by the Allison Engine Company in Indianapolis, Indiana. The engine had ridden into battle on the P-40 Warhawk and the P-51 Mustang, engaged in countless dogfights with German ME-109s and Japanese Zeros. Now it was bolted up to a tractor transmission and winning the 1971 points title in the Modified division. The same power-to-weight ratio that made it a great warrior of the sky made it a great warrior in the dirt.

These engines were designed and built with the idea that failure in the skies over Europe and the Pacific could cost a man his life. They were known for their reliability. In addition, with over 70,000 of them produced, the engines were reasonably affordable and easy to come by, as aircraft engines go.

Ralph Chamberlin rode the old warrior to a 12,000-pound Grand National title in 1970. Bob Bend and Fred Mende of Illinois—"Bend and Mende"—followed Chamberlin's success in 1972 with a 9,000-pound win. They would not be the last to use this venerable power plant.

In this early period of rapid growth, as pullers sought more power, the term "stock" in tractor pulling began to lose its traditional meaning. In some ways, the tractor might look as it did when it left the factory, but the engine was putting

on a lot of muscle. Noble Harrison of Pittsfield, Illinois, pushed the envelope further when he brought two-stage turbocharging to the sport in 1972 in his Allis-Chalmers 220. The outlet of the first turbo was the inlet for the second, giving the engine more air and therefore greater power. Other pullers soon followed, and in 1973 the Super Stock division

was born. No longer farm tractors, these were temperamental beasts that would be no more comfortable on the back 40 than a New York City stockbroker. People had entered tractor pulls with working field tractors for decades, and still do today, but to the greater public, the sport was moving steadily away from the old "pull on Sunday, plow on Monday" concept.

A problem developed, however: With more air and fuel crammed into the combustion chamber, explosions were getting hotter, and engines were just plain melting. This difficulty was so frustrating that J. R. Heriot of Illinois turned to alcohol—for tractor fuel, that is. Alcohol burns colder, which helps lower engine temperature. Heriot built a tractor called *Solid Junk*, Dave Stangle drove it, and the first "alky" was born.

HYPER-STAGING

In 1972, with the sport in a period of rapid growth, an engineering genius with a penchant for power and International Harvester (IH) tractors opened shop. The business was called Hypermax, and the man with all the good ideas on how to coax more power from a red Super Stock tractor was Jerry Lagod. Lagod's genius had a tremendous impact on Super Stock pulling and helped fuel an era of dominance for International Harvester tractors.

John Thompson drove the first pulling tractor with Hypermax engineering under the hood. It was an IH 1466 with a two-stage turbocharger and the first water-injection intercooling system in the sport. Lagod's intercooler lowered

Dave Stangle drove the first alky, called *Solid Junk*, the creation of J. R. Heriot of Illinois. Something of an oddity at the time, alcohol-fueled tractors eventually needed a separate division of pulling. As shown in this photo, Stangle put a sign on the front of his tractor that read, "Watch out for flying parts." *NTPA*

air temperature after the first pressure stage, without restricting flow, allowing downstream components to hold up under greater inlet pressure. Without the water-cooling system, the intense heat generated by the turbo tended to melt downstream engine parts like ice cream in the summer sun.

Thompson's tractor was nicknamed *Silver Shields,* as the engine was hidden behind sheet metal, a new innovation in style. Many other pullers have sheeted over the engine and painted it with murals, but Thompson's was the first.

After one look at Thompson's machine, every owner of a red IH tractor wanted to talk to Jerry Lagod. Pullers like Danny Dean of Ohio and Dickie Sullivan of Missouri soon adopted Hypermax.

The battle lines began to clear in the Stock divisions, and each army had a different color. It was great for the fans. For many of them, allegiance to a manufacturer and color was a way of identifying with pullers. However, these would be hard years for Super Stock fans who did not prefer the color red,

John D. Thompson of Marshall, Indiana, is shown here on his IH 1466 Super Stock tractor, *Bad Dog.* Thompson was the first puller to enjoy the fruits of Hypermax's advanced tractor engineering—a two-stage turbocharger combined with a water-injection intercooling system. *NTPA*

Art Arfons of Akron, Ohio, is credited with bringing the gas turbine engine to the sport of tractor pulling. Arfons gained experience with turbines while setting the land speed record on the Bonneville Salt Flats in Utah. He and Bob Frock of Ohio used that experience to build the first turbine-powered Modified tractor in 1974. *NTPA*

particularly in the heavier classes. With Hypermax designs and the financial backing of corporate headquarters, IH became a true dynasty in the 1970s and 1980s.

Meanwhile, the seeds of another dynasty were sprouting in northern Indiana, as the Banter brothers began their astounding dominance of tractor pulling. The Banters' string of Grand National championships eventually extended to 22, a feat so unbelievably difficult it will probably never be matched. NTPA officials had to order Banter trophies so many times they just reused the same form and scratched in a new year.

To some extent, the Banters' fortunes were furthered in 1973 by Carl and Paul Bosse, two brothers from Ohio, trying to figure out a way to get more horsepower on board their Modified tractor. Of course, adding another engine would do the trick, but how? Searching his memory, Carl recalled that in the military he had seen a tank driven by two Cadillac engines rigged together with a cross-box.

Carl Bosse's idea sparked a minor revolution in tractor pulling. It began with the Bosse brothers' dual-powered Modified tractor, which took the 1973 Grand National points title in the heavy class with four 460-ci Ford engines cranking in harmony. Modified tractor development took a sharp left turn that year and just kept going. If you could harness two engines with a cross-box, why not three, four, six, or eight? Before long, the sport saw many of these configurations. Modifieds soon became multiengine machines, their V-8s harnessed like so many Clydesdales before the cab. As more power was sought, more horses were hitched to the wagon.

And while multiengine tractors ruled the Modified division thereafter, the process of building a winning tractor with sets of engines became an art form for Ralph and Dave Banter.

They liked to lay out their trademark Chevy 427 engines first, achieving tractor balance right from the start. Then they built the frame around the engines. The Banters were out-horsed on many occasions over the years, but when it came to putting the whole package together and running it down the track, they usually made it farther than anyone else.

While the added engine horsepower was a pleasant surprise to fans, it was an unhappy one for the rest of the drivetrain. Rear end failure became a common problem throughout the circuit, as the old tractor rear ends groaned and shattered under the strain. Many pullers smoothed the power path with truck differentials married up to heavy outboard planetaries, which brought the increased twist to the wheels without leaving the transmission in ruins.

TAKING FLIGHT

Power path management became an issue for a completely different type of Modified tractor in 1974. That year saw the emergence of Art Arfons, another legend of the sport. Arfons set the land speed record with a turbine engine on the Bonneville Salt Flats in Utah and became interested in tractor pulling.

He and Bob Frock of Ohio introduced the first jet-propellant-fueled, gas-turbine-powered tractor to the sport—in the obviously and completely Modified division. The gas turbine was a radically different type of power plant, and its tremendous power-to-weight ratio gave it some advantages on the pulling track. Plus, there was always the possibility that Arfons would bolt on a couple of wings and take the thing airborne.

Arfons took the NTPA Grand National title in 1979, sandwiched between wins at Indy in 1978 and 1980 in the 12,200-pound class. His success firmly established the turbine as a viable tractor pull engine.

Meanwhile, by the mid-1970s the other aircraft engine, the Allison V-12, was a staple of tractor pulls. And while it

It's hard to imagine the history of pulling without thinking of the Banter brothers. It's more than just their accomplishments, it's the way they competed, and the way they worked in the shop.

The two brothers from La Fontaine, Indiana, ended up with 22 Grand National

The Banter Brothers

titles and 12 Indy Super Pull wins, but what comes to mind when many pullers think of them is their relentless competitive spirit. They didn't win every event they entered, but they sure tried.

The Banters started out with a tractor that cost about $75. Over the years, they ran 40 different tractors down the track. Some were redesigns, but they all amounted to an effort to make what worked a little bit better—an effort to figure out what was really making the difference, and then make that difference even bigger. The Banters were never satisfied with a great tractor or a win. They wanted to do it again.

From the beginning, Ralph turned the wrenches and Dave drove, and by sticking to that formula, they stayed out of each other's way—often an issue among brothers.

Their different personalities were perfectly matched to their roles. Ralph is four years older, more conservative and rational. He made sure the equipment was up to the challenge. Dave complemented him by providing that challenge and driving hell-for-leather at the wheel.

"If Ralph drove," Dave Banter told The Puller late in his career, "he would be worrying about a spider gear, or a rear end, and wouldn't go as hard. I make a better driver than Ralph because all I worry about is just hammering down."

At the same time, without someone to really sweat the strength and capability of that spider gear or rear end, something usually gives, the tractor spins out short, no matter who's at the wheel.

They needed each other, and they were lucky in that sense. Even though most of the cheers were directed at Dave, he was the first to point them in the direction of his brother. "It's Ralph's stuff," he said. "I'm just drivin' it. If I'd tried to keep up with it, there's no way we'd be where we are today. Ralph is definitely the one who's got us where we are today."

Although the Banters were consistent winners, they were never afraid of trying something new. They went with a rear engine tractor one year—it flopped. They mounted Dave sidesaddle on the tractor, perched off to the right, in front of the rear tire—no go. In the late 1970s, they hired Bill Noland to drive, and sandwiched him in between the two engines up front.

That spirit of experimentation kept them fresh, kept them learning. But according to Dave, they always came back to the basics. "Whenever I moved out from between the tires, it was a mistake. To get the feel of the tractor, you've got to sit between those tires."

Underneath it all, it was hard work and common sense that kept the Banters on top, like Dave's basic approach to reading the track. "If the guy in the lead is an early guy, or if the distances are falling down, you look for a new track. If they are getting better and better, they're building a road. And you better follow that road."

The Banter brothers ran 40 different tractors down the track, including this one at the Indy Tractor Pull in 1989. *Photo Joe Egli*

was increasingly challenged by multiengine tractors, at 1,710 ci, it was still a monster of an engine. Its dominance, particularly in the heavy classes of Modified tractors, was apparent in the performances of pullers like Ron Barga.

Barga launched a four-year run of Grand National titles for Allison engines in 1975, taking six of the eight heavy-class championships himself.

Allison engines were also dominant among the bigger Modifieds at the first Indy Super Pull, held at the Indiana

State Fairgrounds in 1974. Bob Bend won the inaugural event in the 9,000-pound class, and in 1976, E. J. Potter, Ralph Chamberlin, and Dave Haley all rode Allisons to Modified tractor victories; Bud Wheeler and Norm Smith added more in 1977.

But the Modified division of pulling was moving in two directions. It was getting bigger, with gas turbine engines and Allison V-12s, and it was getting smaller, too. In 1974, the Modified Mini division was born at 1,500 and 1,700 pounds. This division of pulling allowed all the ingenuity and imagination of the Modified class, but in a smaller package.

The elimination of the pace tractor in 1974 also had a lasting effect on the structure of the competition. This was an important step, although not everyone realized it at the time. By removing the pace tractor, pulling speeds were no longer governed, leading to a change in approach for the man at the tractor wheel.

The pace tractor moved alongside the pulling tractor at a set speed. The pulling tractor was supposed to stay even with the pace tractor, but pullers had long before figured out a way to build sled momentum and use it as an edge in competition. They took advantage of the pace tractor by either faking it out at the start—getting it to start first—or drifting behind it early in the pull.

"What you did," Dave Banter explained in later years, "was you let the pace tractor get a little ahead of your pull tractor. Then you opened up your throttle in order to catch up. By so doing, you moved that sled a little faster so it would 'work' for you, and not against you."

With the pace tractor gone, tractor jockeys now strove to build forward momentum off the line, before the load

Ron Barga of Ansonia, Ohio, passes the 150-foot mark. Barga dominated the heavy classes (9,000 pounds and 12,000 pounds) of Modified tractors on the Grand National Circuit, taking both titles in 1975 and 1976. He chose the Allison V-12 engine for his power plant. Check out the pipe-organ style exhaust. *NTPA*

increased. That momentum could help carry the sled farther down the track. As a result, initial wheel speeds shot up, and the ideal power curve for a pulling tractor began to look more like the side of a mountain than a gentle rolling hill.

THE RED CHARGE

As the decade progressed, among the Super Stocks, International Harvester and Hypermax engineering took charge of the field. Starting in 1977, red took the 9,000-pound class for the next 14 years. Some of the greatest names in pulling battled for this coveted title—men such as Dean, Klug, and Lehn, all behind the IH logo.

Danny Dean of South Charleston, Ohio, was 25 when he won his first Grand National Cham-pionship in the 9,000-pound, Super Stock class. He became famous as the driver of *The Rooster*, a big red IH 1066, and eventually took home 10 Grand National titles in heavy-class competition, as well as five Indy Super Pull trophies.

John Klug from Stockport, Iowa, was next to command the Heavy Super Stocks. He amassed nine Grand National titles and was unbeatable in the mid-1980s, taking four in a row from 1982 to 1985 in the 9,000-pound class, along with four wins at Indy.

Klug's IH 1066 was named *Red Baron*—a good name for a tractor in America, maybe, but one with much heavier over-tones in Europe, as Klug discovered. One year, he and his

wife, Connie, took their tractor to France on a pulling tour. The *Red Baron* competed in the same fields over which its namesake had downed 80 aircraft, and the tractor caused quite a sensation among the locals.

Competing alongside Klug and Dean was Esdon Lehn, of Dayton, Minnesota, who took his first Grand National Championship in 1983 at the age of 27. Lehn started pulling in local farm contests. He kept winning, and kept looking for more competition, and when he found it, for the most part, he just kept beating it. Lehn's career spanned three decades with Grand National championships in each.

While these pullers were turning the Heavy Super Stock competition into an IH awards ceremony, the 5,500-pound Super Stock class, starting in 1976, was becoming the

This photo shows a Banter brothers creation, driven by Bill Noland who is sandwiched between the two Chevy 427s on a Cockshutt chassis. The Banters from LaFountain, Indiana, dominated tractor pulling for decades to an extent rarely seen in any sport. Their 22 Grand National titles stand to this day as the greatest achievement in pulling. *NTPA*

The overwhelming majority of pulling vehicles are piston-engine powered, but fans of the sport have always been fascinated by the exotic nature of the gas turbine pulling tractor.

It's only natural. When you look at the characteristics of the gas turbine engine it

The Turbine-Powered Tractor

would make a great pulling engine. After all, it is the power plant in the U.S. Army's M-1 battle tank, and that thing weighs 63 tons and can hit 45 mph on the straightaway.

Designers and builders like the turbine engine because it has a fantastic power-to-weight ratio compared to piston engines. That was the selling point in its commercial beginnings as the power plant for the ME262, a 500-mile-per-hour fighter in Hitler's Luftwaffe.

The German engineers noted, as did most aircraft manufacturers from that point forward, that you can get a lot more horse-power from a gas turbine engine than a diesel of the same weight, and it's hard to beat for high-end torque.

But over the years, designing a tractor to turn that advantage into a consistent winner on the track has proved difficult. Turbines have certainly won pulling championships, and have made drivers such as Art Arfons

and Gardner Stone famous, but they have not dominated the sport.

The expense of buying and running a gas turbine has been one problem. Another is that gas turbines like a constant load—like a propeller or helicopter rotor—they're not as amenable to quick throttle adjustments.

After Stone took the Grand National title in 2003, powered by four gas turbines, Gardner said in an interview for the November 2003 issue of The Puller, "They (turbines) are very dependent on the track conditions, some of which give us real problems. Also, the breakage on the turbines doesn't occur on the engine, but usually in the rear end. With the automotive piston setup, the problem usually occurs in the engine.

"The turbines have lots of torque, but it all comes at the high end of the rpm scale. It's definitely hard to keep the machines hooked up. Also, there's no way that you can consistently back-peddle the throttle," he added. "The two types of powertrains are so different."

That's an understatement. There are no pistons, cylinders, or cams in a gas turbine engine. It has three main sections: a compressor, a combustor, and a turbine. In fact, there are far fewer kinds of parts in a turbine engine, as its basic operating concept is much simpler.

The compressor mashes the incoming air down into the combustor much like a blower or turbocharger would, but with a much higher pressure ratio. Where a four-stage turbocharger system on a Super Stock tractor might hope for a 14-to-1 pressure ratio at best, some turbines achieve a 30-to-1 increase. (The air pressure at the outlet of the compressor is 30 times ambient air pressure.) The combustor takes this hot, high-pressure air, injects fuel, and burns the mixture in a hollow, perforated container sometimes called a "can."

Needless to say, when the explosion of fuel expands extremely hot, high-pressure air, the result is very high pressure, very high velocity "gas" (the mixture of air and burnt fuel). And this spins the turbine as it rushes past.

Some of the energy of the spinning turbine drives the compressor, and the rest shows up for work—to crank a modified tractor driveshaft or a propeller shaft.

This division of labor for the high-velocity gas is possible because the turbine section is divided into parts. The first part, or set of blades, is locked together on the same shaft as the compressor, and the two spin as one. The second part of the turbine spins free on the output shaft, and drives the vehicle or propeller.

On jet airplane engines, there is no propeller, and thus no output shaft. This leaves a large amount of high-speed gas flying out the back, pushing the plane forward.

Art Arfons runs a turbine-powered tractor at the Hoosier Dome in winter 1984. *Photo Joe Egli*

Don Harness of Dana, Indiana, in *Loud Mouth Lime*, sports three Rodeck engines on his Modified chassis. Harness was among the first pullers to use the Rodeck engine—the first aftermarket, supercharged, aluminum engine block to power a tractor. He used the engine to become the first puller to take two separate Modified classes at Indy with victories in the 7,200- and 9,200-pound classes in 1979. *NTPA*

province of Allis-Chalmers (A-C) and Dennis Brabec. During the next 12 years, A-C tractors won the Grand National 5,500-pound class 10 times, and 7 times it was Brabec who picked up the trophy.

INNOVATIONS CHANGE THE SPORT

Fans were coming and the sport was growing, but it was time for a completely new direction—a revolution in pulling—to keep the momentum. In 1976, tractor pulling acquired an entirely new look as it invited four-wheel-drive (4WD) trucks into the fold. The addition was successful from the start, as it brought to the show a popular vehicle to which fans could immediately relate, since many of them drove 4WDs to the pull.

The 4WDs would be naturally aspirated—no blowers or turbos. Simplifying the division to that extent kept it more affordable and closer to the fans. And four pulling wheels kept the front end down, giving the competition a distinctive look.

Engine horsepower in pulling tractors was leaping ahead, but the rest of the drivetrain was struggling to catch up. When the clutch pedal popped out, there was often too much twist on the shaft, resulting in cracked and shattered transmission parts. Necessity being the mother of invention, the "slipper" or "automatic" clutch emerged on the market in 1975. With a slipper clutch, a driver could put the tractor in gear without using a clutch pedal. The clutch was actuated by weights on the plate and thrown outward by centrifugal force toward the rim of the clutch as the tractor began to rev. There the two plates were pressed together, and the tractor started to move. Therefore, the clutch locked up tighter at higher rpm, resulting in less slippage.

Coming on the heels of the slipper clutch, the tubular-steel chassis arrived in 1977 in the Modified tractor division. The chassis gave tractors a light, sturdy base, allowing for a

large increase in engine weight. The new alloy frames made pullers feel as if they'd just come off a very successful diet, but not every puller embraced them. The Banters, for example, kept to their channel-steel, wedge-type frames.

Meanwhile, in the Super Stock division, Norm Green, with Bob Mitchell and Al Kock, finally reached the aspiration limit for Super Stock tractors. They put together four turbochargers ahead of the air inlet, and the resulting power became a force to be reckoned with.

RODECK REVOLUTION

Around this time, Bruce Hutcherson and Don Harness, both of Indiana, decided to try a popular drag racing engine in their Modified tractors. They introduced the Rodeck engine to the sport of tractor pulling—the first aftermarket supercharged aluminum engine block to power a tractor. Harness was no stranger to the winner's circle. He had cleaned up the circuit at the 5,200-pound level after 1975, and in 1977 won his first Indy Super Pull title in the 7,200-pound class, as

Here is a rare glimpse of the construction of a Modified tractor. This is Bruce Hutcherson's machine, *Makin' Bacon Special*, being laid out in the shop. Note the classic tubular steel chassis. Hutcherson invested about $150,000 on this tractor, including $125,000 for the 524 Rodeck engines. *NTPA*

well as a Grand National title in the 9,200-pound class. Before he was done, Harness earned three more Grand National titles.

The sport felt the influence of the Rodeck engine immediately. With the drag racing power plant up front, Harness became the first puller ever to take two separate Modified classes at Indy, with victories in the 7,200- and 9,200-pound classes in 1979.

Both Harness and Hutcherson were armed with Rodeck engines, and their duels were legendary. Hutcherson won the Grand National points title in 1979 in the 5,200-pound class, and then astounded the pulling world with six Grand National titles in 1981 and 1982, a period of intense, multiclass domination without parallel up to that point in tractor pulling history.

Other pullers took notice. Rodeck was aboard the winning Modified tractor seven times in the five years at the Indy Super Pull, and two more times on a Modified Mini. And in that period, Rodeck-powered tractors brought home 11 Grand National titles.

Dave Schreier of Norwalk, Wisconsin, drives his JD 4320 *Green Power Special II*. Schreier won the 1980 Super Stock Grand National championship in the 7,500-pound class. He later became president and CEO of World Pulling International. This photo was taken in Cedar Rapids, Iowa, in 1979. *NTPA*

CHAPTER 3

Dickie Sullivan of Naylor, Missouri, drives his Super Stock International Harvester 3688, dubbed *War Eagle,* equipped with all four turbochargers allowed by NTPA rules. Sullivan is shown here in 1985, the year he took his third Grand National title. *War Eagle* came on strong late in that year and won its final five 12,200-pound Super Stock competitions on the GNPC circuit. *NTPA*

The 1980s— Classic Confrontations

In the 9,000- and 12,000-pound (later the 11,200-pound) classes of Modified tractors, the 1980s were marked by a monumental three-way battle for dominance in the Modified Heavyweight class. It featured the Banter brothers and their Chevy engines, Bruce Hutcherson with his Rodeck engines, and later in the decade, Tim Engler with Arias engines, all struggling for the top. The Banter brothers had the first and last word. They won the Grand National points titles in 1980 and 1989, and took four straight from 1983 to 1986. Still, Engler and Hutcherson each took back-to-back titles within the decade, and between 1986 and 1988, Engler had almost everybody running for cover in almost every class. He won an almost unbelievable 10 Grand National Championships in those three years.

It was a battle of individual personalities as much as a battle of technologies. The Banters relied on standard Chevy 427 engine blocks, the number of which varied by the year and weight class. Engler got his power from Arias Hemi aluminum block motors, removing and rearranging to meet the different weight limits as well. From the beginning of the decade, Arias engineering was on the rise, first under Ronnie Reed in the Light Modified class, and then in Engler's *Mission Impossible*. These great contests became pulling legend in the years to come.

Part of a long and illustrious pulling career, 1985 was a great year for Ronnie Reed, Longford, Kansas, as he took Grand National Championship in the 5,200- and 7,200-pound classes. That year he won seven out of ten Grand National events in the 5,200-pound class, taking second in the other three. This photo depicts Reed in an earlier, less technically sophisticated era. *NTPA*

NEW DIVISIONS, NEW FANS

While already a crowd favorite in many competitions around the country, the Two-Wheel-Drive (2WD) division was recognized by the NTPA in 1983. Its first champion, in both the 5,800- and 6,200-pound classes, was Glenn Smith in a Chevrolet. The question at the end of the season was already in the minds of many pulling fans: How did Glenn steer down the track all summer with the front end in the air?

Pullers try to get the most out of their tractors by adjusting horsepower to raise the front end slightly. That puts all the weight on the rear wheels, maximizing traction. Just like other pulling vehicles, the 2WDs have independent rear wheel brakes. By braking the wheel opposite the direction of the turn and allowing the other wheel to catch

In 1987 Danny Dean brought his red International Harvester, *Rooster*, to the place where championships are won. Dean, from South Charleston, Ohio, drove this Super Stock 9,500-pound tractor to glory the following year at the Indy Super Pull. *NTPA*

up, the 2WD pulling trucks can generally maneuver down the track without going out of bounds. It's a necessary evil, of course, as braking of any kind is not good for distance during a pull.

Boundaries define a pulling division as much as a pulling track. By putting limits on the allowable equipment for the Super Stock division, the sport created a completely new field of competition.

Prostock tractors were like Super Stocks, but limited to one inlet pressure stage, and restricted to stock blocks and stock transmission housings, among other components.

In part, they addressed a persistent problem in the sport—keeping pulling affordable for the pullers.

The first year for Prostocks at Indy was 1983, although the NTPA had already recognized the division for two years. That year, John and Mike Linder from Edison, Ohio, took control of the division with Grand National titles in both the 10,000- and 12,200-pound classes. The Linder brothers went on to take the next three heavy titles in a row, finishing their run in 1986. Fifteen years later, they returned for a dominating encore performance, winning in Louisville and taking the 2001 Grand National championship.

Pictured is John Klug on *Red Baron*, winning the Indy Super Pull at the Indiana State Fairgrounds Coliseum January 17, 1987. It was the first year the Indy Super Pull was co-sanctioned by the NTPA and TNT. At the event, Klug added wins in the 11,200- and 9,500-pound smokers division to his long list of pulling championships.
Photo Joe Egli

Nineteen eighty-three was also the year that Esdon Lehn took his first Grand National points championship in the Super Stock 7,500-pound class, and launched a series of GNP championships under the red sheet metal of the International Harvester Corporation. Between Lehn, Bill Berg, and Rob Russel, six of the next seven 7,500-pound Grand National points champions were IH-borne. In the heavier 9,000-pound class, IH had already been master of the track for some time.

BIG IRON DUEL

The year 1986 typified the classic "big iron" duels for mastery of the Modified class. The midwinter competition at the State Fair Coliseum in Indianapolis gave some indication of the season to come, as Engler and the Banters split the Modified class titles. For the first time in the history of the Indy Super Pull, Engler won both light classes, while the Banters took both heavies. In that year, Engler and the Banter brothers finished either first or second in the Grand National 7,200-, 9,200-, and 11,200-pound classes, and Engler had the 5,200-pound class to himself.

Tim Engler drives the Arias Hemi aluminum engine-powered *Mission Impossible*, at the Louisville Championship Tractor Pull, Saturday, February 12, 1988. In the period from 1986 to 1988, Engler won a spectacular 10 Grand National championships in the Modified division: the 5,200-pound class title (1986, 1987); the 7,000-pound class title (1986, 1987, 1988) the 9,200-pound class title (1987, 1988); and the 11,200-pound class title (1986, 1987, 1988). *Photo Joe Egli*

The Banter brothers were working on a string of titles in the 9,200-pound class which stretched back to 1983, longer than that among the 11,200-pounders. But as Ralph Banter said before the start of the pulling season, "They've been gunning for me for years; that's what has kept it interesting." The brothers knew the year would be the most competitive they'd ever seen.

Their formidable five-engined *Orange* was joined by *Brown*, a tractor with six Chevies pulling out front. These two Banter tractors battled Engler's *Mission Impossible* all

summer, from Cayuga to Tomah to Columbus, where a disastrous mechanical failure left Engler out of the top 15, and all but awarded the 7,200-pound class trophy to the Banter boys. Or so people said. By mid-August, as the trailers rolled into Bowling Green, with only four pulls to go, the Banters led by a mountainous 22 points in the 7,200-pound class, and by 13 in the 9,200-pound class.

That lead in the hands of a weaker pulling team might have left Engler a glimmer of hope. But these were the Banters. They wouldn't crack—they'd been through this kind

Dave Banter goes for a full pull at the Grundy County Agricultural Fairgrounds north of Morris, Illinois, June 30, 1988. Banter went up against John Hileman and Bill Leischner that night in the 7,000-pound Modified class. With two tractors entered, Banter won both first and second place with the only two full pulls of the contest. *Photo Joe Egli*

Shown here in 1985, Dennis Horst of Chambersburg, Pennsylvania, sports Arias power in his mini-Modified *Red Fox.* Horst won the 1984, 1991, and 1992 NTPA Grand National Championship, and was runner-up from 1987 to 1989. He went on to win three straight Grand Nationals from 1997–1999. *NTPA*

After seeing just one pull in 1972, Ronnie Reed and his wife were hooked on the sport. They put together a Modified tractor and pulled for five Grand National titles (1980, 1983, 1984, and two in 1985) and three Indy Super Pull wins (1982, 1984, 1985). A true legend of the sport, Reed is shown here driving the Arias-powered *Nemesis. Photo Joe Egli*

John Hileman sits atop his Rodeck-powered machine at the Christian County Fairgrounds in Taylorville, Illinois, on Friday night, July 15, 1988. "This is one of the nicest little pulls we have ever been to," he said of Taylorville. "One hundred five degrees this afternoon and they fed us fried chicken in an air-conditioned building. What more could you ask for?" *Photo Joe Egli*

of pressure many times before. Still, in the great Ohio event, Engler chipped six points off the Banter lead among the 7,200-pounders. A week later in Des Moines, Banter was poised to resume the duel, but where was Engler? The clock ticked slowly and steadily toward the first hook, and there was no sign of the blue and white Modified tractor—or its driver.

At the last possible second, Engler roared into the parking lot. He'd had trouble with his over-the-road hauler. Working quickly, Engler got his machine in position and went the full distance twice to take the Unlimited as well as the 7,200-pound class, knocking another eight points off the Banters' lead. It was down to eight points with two weeks to go.

Mike and John Linder form the famous Linder brothers Prostock pulling team from Edison, Ohio. Mike was 32 years old when this photo was taken in 1986. It shows the brothers' John Deere 4320 in the process of winning its fourth straight NTPA Grand National title, this one in the 12,000-pound class. *NTPA*

Getting the right amount of fuel into a combustion chamber has always been key to maximizing horsepower.

For most of the history of tractor pulling, the carburetor did the job. It worked fine for early pulling machines, and still performs the task at some levels of competition, but where there are tractors battling for big purses and recognition, pumps and injectors are generally the prime movers of tractor fuel.

Carburetors lost their jobs in big pulling tractors for several reasons. For one thing, in a carburetor, air pressure moves the fuel and ambient air pressure has a finite limit. Therefore, it also has a finite flow rate. As tractors became larger and stronger, they demanded more fuel flow. A pump and injector system was needed to add pressure and get more fuel moving.

Another reason for the demise of carburetors in pulling is their float and needle system, which prefers a roughly level orientation to operate properly. Wheel-standing tractors or 2WD trucks interrupt the fuel supply. In a fuel-injected engine, the right amount of fuel is injected individually into each cylinder, regardless of whether the tractor is rearing up or level. Injectors offer more precise control of fuel flow. A fuel injector is an electronically controlled valve, and it reacts in a millisecond to any command, much faster than the carburetor.

The fuel injector system is driven by a pump that runs off the engine, usually the camshaft, which orders and times other engine functions. When the engine speeds up, the pump runs faster and creates more pressure and flow, thereby supporting the higher rpm. In the system, fuel is measured out by a metering valve into a distribution block and then forced through the nozzles. Fuel delivery is tailored to the exact mix by diverting and returning some of the fuel to the tank.

When the injector is actuated, at just the right instant, a solenoid opens the valve, allowing the pressurized fuel to squirt out through a tiny nozzle. The nozzle is designed to atomize the fuel—to turn it into a fine mist so it will burn easily. The mix is important. The explosion in a cylinder is the chemical reaction of a

Fuel Injection

precise amount of fuel and a precise amount of air. When the proportions are perfect, the fuel and air are burned completely, and there's practically none left over. If there's excess fuel vapor, it's stealing airspace and restricting burning. Not enough fuel, and the tractor is again producing less horsepower than it can.

The air pressure and density affect the fuel mixture, too. When air pressure and density go down, the amount of fuel going into the combustion chamber must be reduced accordingly to keep power maximized. Many factors can cause lower air pressure and density. High ambient temperatures often have that effect. A coming storm or a climb in altitude can lower air pressure. Even a high level of pollutants in the air will reduce the oxygen available to be mixed, compressed, and burned in an engine cylinder. In all of these cases, excess fuel in the combustion chamber will actually decrease power, as well as waste gas, preventing the engine from performing at its peak.

At Fort Recovery the following week, Engler was practically unstoppable. Only Bruce Hutcherson's monumental effort in the 7,200-pound class, edging *Mission Impossible* by a mere 3 feet, kept Engler from winning all four Modified weight classes.

One final contest would decide the issue, and all eyes turned to Lincoln, Nebraska, in the last days of August 1986. The Banters' lead in the 9,200-pound class was solid, as was Engler's in the Unlimited and 5,200-pound class. But of the Banters' 22-point lead in the 7,200-pound class coming out of Columbus, just five points remained.

Engler. And he charged right through. Engler won the class with a full pull, joining his buddy Bruce Hutcherson as the only pullers ever to take three Grand National titles in the same season.

Later, after the dust had settled and the crowd was breaking up, Dave Banter showed up at Engler's trailer. He was holding a bottle of champagne. With a five-point lead, he'd bought the bubbly for his own victory celebration. "But it didn't work out that way," he said, "so I'm gonna celebrate with you."

As Engler said later, "It took a heck of a man to come over and do that."

TRUCK TITLES

It is always the human side of the sport that captures the fans. Men who compete like devils on the track can always be found together late at night, sharing a drink and a laugh. And no sport boasts the family ties of pulling. In the late 1980s another set of brothers emerged into the bright lights of pulling fame: the Holmans, Jim and Paul, from Wauseon, Ohio. Younger brother Jim was just 29 when the team took its first title in their famous Chevy, *4 Play*.

In 1989, they won both the light and heavy 4WD Grand National titles, and followed that up with two straight 6,200-pound class titles in 1990 and 1991. After this impressive run, they continued to be a force on the track, winning four more Grand National titles by 2001.

The trackside buzz went straight to the point: For Engler to have a chance, the Banters would have to come in sixth or lower. Tension heightened when the Banters' *Brown* struggled, dropping in the standings and leaving the door open for

Paul Holman, Wauseon, Ohio, sits behind the wheel of *4 PLAY.* Along with brother Jim Holman, the pulling team brought home eight NTPA Grand National titles in the 4WD class. Paul was 31 years of age when this photo was taken in 1987. A year later, the brothers began winning championships. *NTPA*

Stan Johnson rides *Rawhide*, his John Deere tractor, which finished second in the NTPA points race in the 12,000-pound Prostock class and fifth in the 10,000-pound class in 1987. Johnson won the Louisville Championship Tractor Pull twice. "You know," he admitted once, "building the winning tractor is more important to me than driving it." *Photo Joe Egli*

Esdon Lehn of Dayton, Minnesota, pulled his way to two Super Stock class wins at the Grundy County Agricultural Fair in 1988. John Klug, Bill Voreis, and retired pulling great Johnny Bockwitz were also at the pull. Lehn had the only two full pulls of the evening. *Photo Joe Egli*

As for the trucks that only pull with two wheels, another championship family was getting started. L. D. Nation of Pleasanton, Kansas, was piling up wins in the Grand National circuit on his way to his first points title. He took both weight classes in 1989, and with his son, Brent, the single 6,200-pound title the next three years, completely dominating the division.

Eight years later, Craig Nation began to add to the family glory with three out of four 2WD titles, starting in 2000.

Pulling legend Dennis Brabec is shown here at Kankakee, Illinois, in 1988, on his way to a full pull aboard his A-C *Imposter,* a 7,000-pound Super Stock tractor. Brabec won the Indy Super Pull in 1977, 1979, 1983, and 1985, and along with brother Allan, formed the Brabec Brothers Pulling Team. They took the Grand National title seven times to the delight of Allis-Chalmers Super Stock pulling fans. *Photo Joe Egli*

L. D. Nation pulls at the Iowa State Fairgrounds, August 21, 1991. There were 8,800 pulling fans in attendance to watch 17 trucks in the 2WD division competition, won by Nation in *Bad Medicine*. He was leading the NTPA points race at the time, and finished that way, winning his third Grand National out of four. *Photo Joe Egli*

CHAPTER 4

Dave Banter sits on *Bandit* at the Iowa State Fairgrounds in Des Moines, Iowa, August 23, 1991. In the Unlimited final, Banter and Rodalyn Knox both pulled the full distance, leaving Gardner Stone and Ronnie Reed in third and fourth place. Banter recaptured the NTPA points lead (and later the championship itself) with a win over Knox's blown, Hemi-powered *Country Girl*. *Photo Joe Egli*

The 90s—Shifting Gears

The sport of tractor pulling saw enormous change in the 1990s, in everything from structure to technology. The venerable Indy Super Pull simply shut its doors, never to be heard from again. At the same time, a new pull organizer, the American Tractor Pullers Association (ATPA), opened for business, with plans for big pulling purses and TV contracts.

Changes in technology had dramatic effects on horsepower, pulling divisions, and rules. As the decade began, turbine power was again arousing interest in many high-profile pulls. The year before, in 1989, Gardner Stone introduced *The General Stage IV,* a Modified tractor with four gas turbine engines spinning, a formidable machine, and Art Arfons was continuing his competitive run in *Green Monster.*

With an Unlimited Modified Grand National championship in 1990, Stone re-ignited, at least temporarily, the long-standing debate between turbine power and piston power advocates. And there were plenty of these. The piston-driven Banters were still in the thick of the pull, and they started the 1990s behind six Chevrolet engines in *Mr. Chevy.*

The Indy Super Pull January 11–13, 1991, brought together Stone and the Banters in a memorable setting. The venue that had hosted some of pulling's greatest competitions was in its final years. The event had, in fact, been canceled the year before due to scheduling problems.

In the 7,200-pound Modified class, under the lights at the Indiana State Fairgrounds Coliseum, Stone and the Banters dueled for the top three spots. The Banters took two of them, but Stone brought home the trophy.

The surprise of the entire season came on the final day of competition in the Unlimited class. Rodalyn Knox, in her first appearance at Indy, rode her KB hemi-powered mod, *Sassy Massey*, 2 inches farther than Tim Engler to become Indy's first woman Modified winner.

"I have to keep pinching myself to make sure I'm not dreaming," she said after the pull. Her win at Indy capped an astonishing rookie season. Competing in 14 Grand National events, Knox won four of them and placed second five times. Some might have imagined that in a male-dominated sport, her performance would have evoked some hard feelings from other drivers. Not so, Knox told *The Puller* after her big year. "I didn't know how [the other pullers in the Modified division]

Art Arfons lit up in flames at the Rosemont Horizon in Chicago during the SRO-Pace Promotions shootout. On Saturday night, February 10, 1990, Arfons and his twin turbine-powered *Green Monster* took second in the Modified division behind Steve Jaske and his five blown Arias engines. *Photo Joe Egli*

were going to take me," she said. "But they were just the best. Everybody was so friendly."

Knox went on to win the Grand National Championship in the Unlimited class, which eluded her in her rookie season, a total of three times. Those victories included back-to-back titles in 1997 and 1998.

RISE AND FALL

The organization of the pulling world also underwent fundamental change in 1991. A competitor to the NTPA was born that year, when the American Tractor Pullers Association (ATPA) was founded in Charlestown, Indiana. The ATPA focused on trying to build the pop-

ularity of the sport in a variety of ways, and provided the structure for great pulling competitions in its own right.

While the ATPA was taking root and growing, the last wintertime pulls were hooking up in Indianapolis. There were still some thrills in store for fans who braved the snowy weather, however.

The 1993 Indy Super Pull was a particularly memorable one for many pullers. Nine of the 15 Super Stock smokers pulled the entire 300 feet on the first round that year, but it was Esdon Lehn on *Red Line Fever*, just 5 inches short of his second full pull, who took the 7,500-pound Super Stock Indy title. Warren Ropp won the heavy class in his John Deere *Big Green Machine*.

In the 4WD class, the Holman brothers were looking for their first win at Indy. Despite their dominance of the 4WD Grand National circuit, they'd been completely shut out at the

coliseum, having come agonizingly close in 1991. That year, Jim Holman drove *Enterprise Machine* hard, but came up 2 inches short of a pull by Ed Hanslovan of Pennsylvania. In the next-to-last 4WD pull-off at Indy, it was down to a Ford driven by Lem Freday of Missouri, and the Holmans' Chevy. The two competitors fought the sled most of the way down the track, but when the dirt had settled, the Holmans had finally broken through at the Indy Super Pull.

Meanwhile, in the Modified division, a great story was shaping up—the kind that makes the sport of tractor pulling different from every other motor sport—a father-daughter duel on the track. Art Arfons, the granddaddy of turbine pulling power, was back at Indy with two big gas turbine engines out front. And so was his daughter, Dusty. When the whine of the aircraft engines subsided, and fans checked the scoreboard, they discovered there had been two full pulls in

John Hileman of Rockford, Ohio, sits aboard *Ohio Gold* at the National Farm Machinery Show and Championship Tractor Pull in Louisville, Kentucky, February 1991. Hileman won four Grand National Modified titles in the late 1970s and early 1980s. *Photo Joe Egli*

Gardner Stone from Middlebury, Vermont, drives *The General Stage IV*. This photo was taken in 1990, a year before he won both the 7,200-pound and Unlimited Modified Grand National championships. He won again in 2003 (his fourth title) with four Lycoming turbines still up front. *Photo Joe Egli*

the 7,200-pound Modified class, and both drivers had the last name Arfons.

A pull-off would decide which one would take the coveted prize. Imagine the feelings of a father, lining up against his daughter in front of nearly 10,000 fans, with so much at stake. Dusty went 230 feet, 7 inches in the pull-off, and then it was up to Art. He sat on his tractor, hooked to the sled, motionless, for what seemed like forever. The crowd waited, squirming with anticipation, minute after minute, as Arfons simply sat on his tractor without moving. Tension mounted to a fever pitch. And still, Arfons remained in his seat. Finally, he reached up, shut down his machine, and climbed down off the *Green Monster*. Turbine No. 2 had failed to fire. The new-generation Arfons had the title.

Another fitting finale matched the Banters against the turbine-powered Gardner Stone and rising star Rodalyn Knox. Throughout the early 1990s, the Banter team was still in the thick of the competition with two tractors, *Mr. Chevy* and *Bandit*, each with six supercharged Chevy 454s ripping down the track in the Unlimited division.

Their tractor-building business was still booming, and sometimes served as a place where good pulling relationships were forged, in addition to a good pulling chassis. Knox herself got to know the Banters after going to their shop for technical help in her rookie season.

Of course, when the sled is hooked up out on the track, even friends and relatives become rivals. And despite warm feelings, the Banters took their 10th Indy title in the 8,200-pound Modified class that year, narrowly edging out Knox, Gardner Stone, and Dave Walsh.

Pulling fans emerged from the Coliseum Sunday night, January 10, 1993, trudging through heavy snow that had fallen the night before. Conflicts with other events scheduled at the Indiana State Fairgrounds Coliseum forced a two-week delay in 1994, and in 1995 put an end to what had been the mother of all pulling events. It was a shock to the pulling

world to lose such a revered, successful event, but a little over 100 miles to the south another pulling venue was coming into its own.

The Championship Tractor Pull in Louisville, Kentucky, had drawn hundreds of thousands of pulling fans to Freedom Hall since 1969, and was a premier event in its own right. With the loss of Indy, however, the spotlight shone even more brightly on the midwinter indoor pull. In 1993, the Championship Tractor Pull in Louisville began awarding the title "Grand Champion" to the winner of a final round of competition on Saturday night at Freedom Hall.

Precisely a month after the 1993 Indy Super Pull, the 25th Championship Tractor Pull (CTP) opened competition in Freedom Hall in Louisville. Over a quarter-million people were on hand for the National Farm Machinery Show, always held next door. In that crowd of farm equipment buyers and sellers were enough pulling fans to pack the stands for four days of pulling.

In 1991, Rodalyn Knox, in her rookie season, won the Unlimited Modified class at the Indy Super Pull. Her KB hemi-powered tractor *Sassy Massey* narrowly edged Tim Engler. In 1995, she began to dominate the circuit, winning three Grand National titles in the following four years in the Unlimited Modified division. *Photo Joe Egli*

Four division trophies were at stake: Prostock, won by Jon Lorenz in *Sneaky Snake*; Super Stock, taken by Mike Goodgine in *The Rattler*; Modified, in which Dave Walsh avenged his near miss a month earlier in *Irish Challenger*; and 2WD Super Modified Truck, won by Richard McPherson in *Missouri Raider*.

Before long, new divisions were added to the lineup. Three classes of Super Stock tractors soon became part of the competition: 7,700-pound Super Stock in 1999; 8,200-pound Super Stock in 2000; and 8,000-pound Super Stock

Alcohol in 2000. In 2002, the show included 9,300-pound Super Farm tractors, and added a 7,500-pound Modified class to the mix.

CHANGING OF THE GUARD

As the spring of 1996 approached, the Modified tractor division was becoming quite a battleground for fading and emerging stars going after the Grand National title in the 7,200-pound and Unlimited classes. Dave Archer of Lowell, Ohio, was the favorite. He had been pulling for 16 years with

Three-time Grand National Unlimited Modified champions Tom and Rodney Martin are from Bonnie, Illinois, where they strike a balance between pulling and the family plumbing and piping business. Their rig is shown here at the NTPA Show Me Show Down in Macon, Missouri, in 1995. *Photo Joe Egli*

Shannon Leischner, son of pulling great Bill Leischner, is shown here in *Dirtslinger T* at Freedom Hall in Louisville in 1996. Shannon won the Louisville Championship Tractor Pull 2WD division that year, his first in pulling, beating out Danny Hubert by four feet. Six years later he won it again in *Dirtslinger*. The Leischners are from Weldon, Illinois. *Photo Joe Egli*

great success in his home state of Ohio, and the previous year he broke through and won the Grand National title in his gleaming *Pioneer* by just two points. The Banter brothers came in second in *Mr. Chevy* in 1995. They had been actively pulling for over 30 years, and after 21 Grand National championships and 31 regional titles, they were looking for one more trophy.

Judy Knipstein of Fort Wayne, Indiana, was also in the running. She had won the Pro National title and the Indy Super Pull twice. She had a nice Engler-built chassis holding up a fine set of Chevrolet engines.

Rodalyn Knox of Weare, New Hampshire, won the Unlimited class Grand National title the previous year in her *Country Girl*, with four supercharged, fuel-injected, 500-ci Dodge Hemis generating 8,000 horsepower. It was the first Grand National title for a woman in the Modified class, and there would be more of them in her future.

Perhaps unnoticed in this group of successful pullers was Bob Jostock, of Lapeer, Michigan. It was his 21st year of pulling sleds, and he'd won the Enderle Pull-Off (a prestigious, qualifiers-only competition between pullers at the top of the points standings in 12 classes held each year in Fort Recovery, Ohio) in 1993, but in 1995 he'd come in eighth place, 51 points off the leader. Jostock mounted four Chevy 454s on his Modified tractor, *Wild Child*, and it became apparent during the season that he now had them dialed in just right.

Amid these established names some fresh faces were rising onto the scene.

One of them was Joe Eder, of North Collins, New York, just 25 years of age. He'd been pulling since he was a teenager and now entered this major competition with *Chevy Thunder*, sporting a Banter/Eder chassis under four 510-ci Chevies. While 1996 would not be his year, sterling victories in the Grand National circuit and the Louisville Championship Tractor Pull lay ahead.

The Martin brothers, Tom and Rodney, were new to the Unlimited Modified circuit as well and getting ready to make a statement. They'd done some Super Stock pulling, but without the results they were looking for, so they resolved to make a change. As Tom put it, "Since we really weren't that competitive at the national level in the Supers, and we were

Esdon Lehn pulls his way to a Grand National win at Davenport, Iowa, on June 14, 1996. With the nose of *Red Line Fever* rising off the Iowa clay, Lehn went out the end on the first hook in the 7,500-pound Super Stock class. So did Matt Goodwin, Tom Dickerson, and Randy Rose. In the pull-off it was all Lehn. *Photo Joe Egli*

spending a lot of money, Rodney and I decided to go the Modified route. We talked to Tim Engler about it and he recommended going with the multiengine heavy classes."

The rest, as the saying goes, was pulling history. The Martins were part of a new group of pullers coming onto the scene, ready to assume the mantle of leadership in the Modified division.

Of the 16 Grand National events that year, several stand out as classic battles. The first was the Mississippi Valley Grand Nationals, in Davenport, Iowa, June 14 and 15, 1996. As the sun went down over the prairie lands to the west, the 7,200-pound Mods hooked up and began to make noise. Joe Eder had his new Banter-built machine with four blown 510-ci Chevies, and Randy Petro, future 2WD Grand National champ, turned up with his multiengine ride, *Multi Chaos*.

Dave Archer, the favorite, roared down the track first and spun out at 250 feet with two blower belts in shreds. After a bit of pit work, Archer was back on the track for another pass. This time the blower locked up entirely, and the spacer plate disintegrated. Trackside, Archer examined his options. He needed a new blower to get back into the pull. He could simply bow out of the competition, or perhaps a long drive and some scrounging might uncover a new one. Dave Banter simply offered Archer one of his.

As so often happens, a graceful act is followed by a graceful performance. Banter proceeded onto the track and yanked the sled 300 feet with ease. Judy Knipstein followed with a full pull as well. Rodney Martin ran the distance right behind her with his four KB Olds motors chugging in tune, but he roasted a head in the process. It came down to Knipstein and Banter for the points. Banter was first up and made it 299.9 feet down the track. Knipstein, with the Iowa crowd and her own team of 526-ci Chevies screaming in her ears, delivered a pull precisely 3 feet farther, for the win.

Art Arfons is on fire, literally, in this photo taken at the 1997 National Farm Machinery Show and Championship Tractor Pull in Louisville. In the first event of the show, Arfons put a little too much air under his front end, got twisted a bit, and then crashed to the ground and burst into flame. That got the crowd fired up, too. *Photo Joe Egli*

In the Unlimited finals Saturday night, there were two full pulls, both driven by Dave Banter—one in *Mr. Chevy* and one in *Bandit*. It was a crucial Grand National win, establishing the Banters early on as the new favorite among the Unlimited Mods.

Two weeks later the competitors found themselves in one of the greatest venues for pulling anywhere—Tomah, Wisconsin. Three days and five sessions of world class pulling followed before an enthusiastic crowd of Badger pulling fans. Sixteen Unlimited Modifieds hooked up the first night, and four of them went the distance—the Martin brothers; Jim Brockmann of New Haven, Indiana; Dave Banter on the *Bandit*; and Art Arfons, on the *Green Monster*. Between the two U.S. Navy helicopter engines, Arfons' tractor could boast over 9,000 horsepower.

The track was lengthened for the pull-off to 310 feet, and the monsters roared again. In the pull-off, the Martin brothers were looking good, but suddenly lost their fire at the

Martin Brothers Motorsports pulling team began operations in 1987, but didn't begin to dominate at the national level until the year 2000. This photo was taken on a beautiful summer day at the Monroe County Fairgrounds in Tomah, Wisconsin, in 1997. "Competition is one of the biggest motivations for us," Tom Martin said in an interview in *The Puller* that year, "To go to an event and win without competition is meaningless." *Photo Joe Egli*

170-foot mark. Brockmann went farther, but the contest came down to Banter and Arfons. It was one of the final opportunities for fans to witness two true legends of the sport in a simple head-to-head pull-off. It was Arfons, the turbine master and crowd pleaser, against the Banters, builders of so many winning tractors over the years. When both tractors had spent themselves in the pull-off, 2 feet separated their pulls. On this night, the turbine blade was stronger than the piston. Arfons took the round, with Banter in second. In the 7,200-pound Modifieds, Randy Petro won the prelims, with Art Arfons 2 feet behind. Judy Knipstein took third behind her Arcola engines, and Rodney Martin was again strong, a harbinger of things to come.

The finals came down to an eight-sided pull-off. Tractor after tractor made a run, but none could match the power of the *Green Monster*. The tractor was digging into the track,

In the preliminary round of the 1998 Louisville Championship Tractor Pull, Esdon Lehn and *Red Line Fever* had the only full pull out of 18 rigs. But in the 7,700-pound Super Stock final, Tadd Eads of Lagro, Indiana, on the *Indiana Rascal* overtook him by less than a foot. Lehn won at NFMS in 1996 and 2003. *Photo Joe Egli*

Hans Boxler Sr., of Varysburg, New York, drives *The Special* at the Louisville Championship Tractor Pull. With Boxler Jr., driving, the team followed with a great showing at the 2004 ATPA Winternationals in the Heavy Super Stock Diesel Tractor class. *The Special,* a fine shiny IH representing the Empire State Pullers, won its preliminary round with a pull of 305.50 feet. Then in the "Sunday Shoot-Out" finals, *The Special* followed the previous evening's victory with the only full pull. Randy DeVaughn, of Gambrills, Maryland, aboard *Road Gear Farmer,* was second at 294.46, while Brian Sharamek's *Young Blood,* from Williamsburg, Missouri, was third. *Kentucky Fair & Exposition Center*

of the top, in a finish filled with past and present stars of the sport. Bob Jostock took the title that year by just three points over Randy Petro, who, for all his efforts, took home second place twice. Judy Knipstein was just a point behind, followed by Dave Banter and Joe Eder.

The previous year's champion, Rodalyn Knox, was not among the leaders, as she spent part of the year recovering from surgery. But Knox went on to win the Grand National title the following two years.

Rising stars Joe Eder and the Martin brothers, on the other hand, climbed into the Modified pulling sky. Two years would see them both champions. In 1997 Eder took the 7,200-pound Modified title, and the Martins won it in 1998.

SEPARATE CIRCUITS, SEPARATE DIVISIONS

As these past and future NTPA champions were passing the championship torch, another Midwestern sanctioning body of tractor pulling was going its own way with its own champions. The split between the NTPA and the ATPA grew bitter in the late 1990s, and pullers and fans were forced to choose sides.

applying its enormous power at the point of friction. Arfons walked away with the Super National win and the bonus purse that goes with it.

Despite Arfons' win at Tomah, by the month of August, consistent performances by the Banters had distanced the rest of the field. They were savoring the likelihood of a final title in the Unlimited class—all the more meaningful after a long career of competition.

But among the 7,200-pound Modifieds, the race was much closer. Five pullers crowded together within 10 points

Scott Smith drives *3 Bears,* with its Edwards-designed engine, in early May 1997. Smith comes from good pulling stock. He is the son of Sara and Bob Smith of Winchester, Virginia, successful 4WD pullers in their own right. Note the door panel paint still proudly displays all three names. *NTPA*

By this time, three major organizations offered top-level pulling events between the Alleghenies and the Rockies: the NTPA, based in Worthington, Ohio; the ATPA, based in Charleston, Indiana; and the Outlaw Truck and Tractor Pulling Association (OTTPA), formed in Springfield, Missouri, some 16 years before.

While the OTTPA was the major organizer west of the Mississippi River, the ATPA and NTPA fought over pulling in the heartland east of the Mississippi. The Louisville Championship Tractor Pull, however, still provided a neutral site for pullers, no matter what letters they ran under. It was a place that could guarantee a large and enthusiastic crowd and a big purse, year after year. And 1998 was no exception.

The 30th Annual Championship Tractor Pull at Louisville's Freedom Hall opened its doors to just under 100,000 pullers and fans for four days of competition. A total purse of $180,000 awaited the winners of five pulling divisions.

This championship was one of the last in which diesel- and alcohol-burning Super Stocks competed head to head on roughly equal footing.

Shown here is Joe Kwiatkowski aboard *Wild Thing* at the National Farm Machinery Show in Louisville in 2000.
In a close finish, Kwiatkowski took second behind Dave Sonnetag, Cadott, Wisconsin, on *Savage*, coming up just 4 feet short. Two years later, Kwiatkowski won the 8,000-pound Alcohol Tractor division at Louisville.
In 2004, he won the ATPA Winternationals in a close match with longtime rival Jordan Lustik. *Photo Joe Egli*

Rivalry had always been intense between fans of alcohol-burning tractors and those burning diesel. Usually it was friendly and good-natured, and sometimes there was an edge to it. But there was no doubt that the alky tractors had made great strides in technology in the 1990s.

Wins had traditionally been rare for alky tractors. An alky won the Grand National title in 1981; and Lyle Hull, of Waupun, Wisconsin, took second in 1987; and Ernie Conner took second again in 1990.

In 1991 and 1992, however, Bryan and Ernie Conner rode their White tractor, *Bad Medicine,* to two straight Super Stock 7,500/9,500-pound Grand National championships, burning nothing but alcohol. With the Connors' back-to-back championships, the gap between alcohol and diesel tractor performance closed.

A seesaw battle raged throughout the mid-1990s as the two technologies traded titles. Richard Lustik and his son, Jordan, drove the alcohol-fueled *Silver Bullet* to Grand National championships in 1995 and 1997 in the 7,500/9,500-pound class. Dogging them every step of the way, Esdon Lehn, Tom Dickerson, and Rob Russell, three IH pullers, had taken three titles for the diesel fans in 1993, 1994, and 1996.

As fans shuffled through the turnstiles at the 1998 CTP, fresh from the National Farm Machinery Show next door, the air crackled with talk of Case IH versus Deere, Ford versus Chevy, and—especially—alky versus diesel.

On the first night of action, the 9,500-pound Super Stocks took to the track. Arnie Kwiatkowski, on his alky *Wild Thing,* kept the sled moving all the way to the sandpile with intimidating ease, but Jordon Lustik, following on the *Silver Bullet,* matched him with his own full pull.

Two diesel tractors came in behind them. Dennis Goodwin on *Magnum Force*, a Case IH tractor, took third, and Eugene Williams on *Buck's Fever* made the cut at fourth.

Bill Vories of Argos, Indiana, on *Orient Express* wins the 7,200-pound Modified class at the 2000 Louisville Championship Tractor Pull. Dave Archer of Lowell, Ohio, the previous year's winner, took second, with Bill Lawrence of Canada third. Vories did well indoors that winter. On January 31 he won the USHRA Monster Jam and TNN Motor Madness Competition—Unlimited Dragster Tractor division—at the Superdome in New Orleans. *Photo Joe Egli*

Although all four made the finals, this round came down to a pull-off between the sons of two great alky Super Stock families—the Lustiks and the Kwiatkowskis. Jordan Lustik's dad, Richard, had roared to glory in the Louisville dirt two years before and took a Grand National title in 1995. Arnie Kwiatkowski's dad, Joe, had won a championship in Louisville, too, and his own Grand National titles in 2001 and 2002. The two pulling teams battled for supremacy in Super Stock pulling across the Midwest for years to come.

On this night, the distance belonged to Arnie. The *Silver* Bullet's Caterpillar engine suddenly gave up halfway down the track, and the *Wild Thing* had the preliminary round win with ease. Both tractors met again in Saturday night's finals. In the other preliminary round, alky tractors won the top two places as another great Super Stock puller, Terry Blackbourn of Shullsburg, Wisconsin, handled *Slowride* to the full pull mark, along with Lawrence Kline Jr. of Ohio on *Green Gate Savage.*

The card was filled. On Saturday night, it was four diesels against four alkies. But in the contest that ensued, the fight

Since 1995 Jordan Lustik and the *Silver Bullet* have won the NTPA Grand National Championship three times—1995, 1997 and 2000. *Silver Bullet* was runner-up in 1999. It prevailed at the Louisville Championship Tractor Pull in 1996 (with Richard Lustik driving), 1998, 2003, and 2004, and it won the ATPA Grand American points championship in 2001, 2002, and 2003. *Don Gillespie*

was really between the tractors burning alcohol. Just 4 feet separated the top three pulls, all alkies, with the rest of the field farther back.

In a glimpse of great pulls in the days ahead, many of them on that very same track in Freedom Hall, Kwiatkowski and Lustik measured within a foot of each other. But it was Lustik's *Silver Bullet* with the win at 238.47 feet. Third place went to Kline Jr.

While most Super Stock tractors in the sport overall had been, and would remain, diesels, this result in Louisville underlined the head-to-head dominance of alcohol-burning tractors in the heavy Super Stock division. Soon diesels needed a separate division to keep competition fair.

The NTPA that year created a diesel-only Super Stock title, and in two years the Louisville Championship had an alcohol tractor title of its own.

The Lustik/Kwiatkowski match-up went on to become legend in Super Stock pulling. Although he lost to Lustik in the finals at Louisville in 1998, Arnie Kwiatkowski went on to capture the Grand National title in the Super Stock open divi-

Roger Simon of Farley, Iowa, in *Simon Sez*, is one of the most consistent performers in all pulling. Simon has won four ATPA championships (1999, 2000, 2001, and 2002), three NTPA championships, (1993, 1997, and 1998), and was runner-up six times. He has also won the NTPA Puller of the Year award and the Simon family has won the Pull Family of the Year award. *Don Gillespie*

sion that year. It was Jordan Lustik in 2000. Then it was Arnie's dad, Joe Kwiatkowski, in 2001 and 2002.

Joe won the 8,000-pound Super Stock Alcohol division at Louisville in 2002, while Jordan took that trophy home in 2003 and 2004. In pull after pull, these Super Stock competitors, joined by 1999 Grand National winner Terry Blackbourn, provided one of the greatest on-track rivalries the sport of tractor pulling has ever known.

While the split in the NTPA Super Stock classification led to the exciting battles between the Kwiatkowskis and the Lustiks, the resulting Super Stock diesel-only class was simply taken over by Esdon Lehn.

Lehn had won his first Grand National Championship 15 years before, at the age of 27. He was a consistent winner from the beginning, eventually counting his Grand National titles in double digits. He won at Indy in 1988, 1990, and 1993. He won in Louisville in 1996 and 2003.

Now, as he entered his early forties, Lehn embarked on a rare string of four straight titles. Five of the next six Diesel Super Stock Grand National titles were Lehn's, too, as he surrendered only the 2002 Grand National to Stan and Steve Blagraves, in perhaps the greatest Grand National finish of all time in Connorsville, Indiana.

GREAT PULLS, GREAT RUNS

Indeed, 1998 was the launchpad for more than one memorable run of titles. Larry Shope of Bellville, Ohio, achieved almost the exact same feat, starting at the exact same time, in the Prostock division. Like Lehn, Shope started his run in 1998 and won five out of the next six Grand National titles in his *Iron Dragon*, a John Deere 4430. If not for a driveline disaster in 2001, he might have run the table. That was the year that John and Mike Linder came out of retirement for one more pull to glory, and won the Grand National for the sixth time.

Joe Eder and his Sorrento Cheese machine were captured in this photo taken in the summer of 2000.
In 2000, Eder ran *Sorrento Express* in the ATPA circuit, taking third place in the final standings with a total of
711 points. Bill Leischner in *Dirtslinger* won with 803 points, and Scott Tedder came in second with 780 on
Mr. Twister. Photo Joe Egli

Cutting Edge, a 2000 Ford Ranger with a 554-ci supercharged alcohol-burning hemi, driven by Stan Shelton of New London, North Carolina, is shown here at the Louisville Championship Tractor Pull. Shelton began pulling at the age of 23 in a 1949 Ford, *The Tom Cat.* In 1996, he began running *Sawmill Express,* named for his wife's family lumber business. In 2000, Shelton added *Cutting Edge,* with which he won the 2003 ATPA 2WD title. *Kentucky Fair & Exposition Center*

Meanwhile, in the Modified Mini division, Dennis Horst was having everything his own way. Horst burned up the track three years running, adding Grand National titles in 1997, 1998, and 1999 to his long list of pulling titles. Horst had also won the Grand National championship in 1984, 1991, and 1992 on his famous *Red Fox*.

And in the 4WD truck division, the Holman brothers were starting a championship tear of their own. The brothers had a long and celebrated pulling history in 4WD trucks, with five Grand National trophies already under glass. Winning again in 1998 seemed to signal a second dynasty, but Scott Smith of Winchester, Virginia, driving the *3 Bears*, challenged this. Smith was emerging from a celebrated past to challenge for the top himself. Smith's dad, Bob, had taken the family's first championship in the *3 Bears* back in 1983. Ten years later, Scott drove the same truck with the same result. And in 1999, to his surprise, Scott and the *3 Bears* did it again. "This one was extra sweet, because the last few years we hadn't been running very good," Smith told *The Puller*. He ran just fine from that point forward.

Following his impressive 2003 ATPA 2WD title, Stan Shelton garnered a dramatic win at the nationally televised ATPA Winternationals. In Friday's initial class run-offs, *Cutting Edge* only made a 286-foot pull, leaving Shelton in sixth place, but qualified for the finals. With some adjustments, the next day Shelton made the only full pull to win the event. "I sure didn't think I'd be in the winner's circle after last night," Shelton said afterward, "but we did our homework, apparently made the right changes." *Don Gillespie*

Mickey Shorter of Sullivan, Indiana, drives the 10,200-pound Prostock *Buck Eater*. The smoker is a 680-ci, turbocharged 6-cylinder diesel John Deere capable of producing well over 1,000 horsepower. Shorter and *Buck Eater* won the Goshen, Indiana, ATPA Grand American on July 25, 2002, beating Tim Sarver in *Green Extreme* in a pull-off, 293 feet to 260 feet. *Don Gillespie*

In the years to come, the battle between these competitors—the Holmans and the Smiths—became a dependable thrill for 4WD truck pulling fans. They split the six Grand National championships from 1998 and 2003 evenly between them.

It couldn't have been any closer in 2003. With two hooks remaining, the Holman brothers held a nine-point lead. But a driveline failure on the Holman brothers' *4-Play* put the *3 Bears* on top by a single point, headed for the last hook of the year in Wauseon, Ohio. Randy Kleikamp in *Old Yeller* was

Greg Hibbitts sits up in the cab of *Pro-Hibbitted*, the beautiful blue CAT-powered Kenworth of the *Pro-Hibbitted* Racing Team. Hibbitts, from Hudsonville, Michigan, owns three Grand National championships. In 2003, the race was a tight battle between Larry Carey of Morley, Michigan, in *Dodge Fever*, J. R. Collins of Painesville, Ohio, in *Buckeye Bulldog,* and Hibbitts, but *Pro-Hibbitted* pulled away from the field at the end, winning four of the last five hooks. *NTPA*

only a point behind the Holmans. Relishing the possibilities, fans of all three pullers packed the country fairgrounds stands for the rare chance to see a single-pull, winner-take-all Grand National title. Tension built with each pull, as Smith, Kleikamp, and Jim Holman awaited their chance at the sled. The air buzzed with amateur strategies as truck after truck spun out short. It seemed that a full pull would win the pull and perhaps the championship, too.

Old Yeller made it—300 feet and more.

And then Scott Smith did, too.

And then Jim Holman joined them with a full pull of his own. Scott Phillips and Jim Bosch, too, cleared the track to spark a five-way pull-off.

Four hooks later, the Grand National title came down to Jim Holman and one pull for the money. Kleikamp was out. Bosch was in first place in the pull-off, and Scott Smith was in second. Win it, and the Grand National title could just stay right there in Wauseon, the Holmans' hometown.

But it was not to be. *4-Play*'s engine knew it before anyone else, as ignition rotor failure slowed the Holman truck, and it came in fourth. Smith had his fourth Grand National title and his first back-to-back championship.

L. D. Nation from Butler, Missouri, pulled at the Dairyland NTPA Super Nationals in Tomah, Wisconsin. After tearing up the circuit in the 2WD division for years, Nation pulled in the Unlimited Modified division with good success. In 2000, when this picture was taken, Nation placed fourth in the points race behind Randy Petro, Bill Voreis, and the Martin brothers. *NTPA*

CHAPTER 5

Kevin Masterson and his father, Don, are grain farmers as well as successful Prostock tractor pullers based in Grandview, Indiana, near the Ohio river. *River Rat,* with Kevin behind the wheel, won the Louisville Championship Tractor Pull in 1997 and the 2000 ATPA Prostock Grand American championship in 2000. *Photo Joe Egli*

Pulling in the New Millennium

As the odometer turned over to 2000, it was time to reflect on the changes that occurred through the years and celebrate the sport's greatest moments. While so many other sports were corrupted beyond all recognition by money and media, pulling's core values remained intact—family, fun, good competition, and sportsmanship. And while some conflicts of allegiance remained between fans and pullers of the ATPA and the NTPA, the fact remained that both sanctioning bodies were providing well-run pulls and great competition.

As proof, the 2000 pulling season offered thrilling races in the Prostock division for both the NTPA Grand National and the ATPA Grand American championships. Alongside a tight contest between Larry Shope and Tim Cain for the NTPA crown, two great pulling families with long histories and multiple tractors—the Mastersons and the Boyds—divided up the top four spots in the ATPA points title.

Families like the Mastersons and Boyds are not unusual in the sport, but they are unusual in the sporting world. They are what separate and dignify tractor pulling. Three generations of the Boyd family have pulled a sled; they started with old stone boats and field tractors and now compete with heavy turbocharged Prostocks and modern weight-transfer machines.

While the equipment has changed, other things have not. There's still an amiable rivalry over brand loyalty. (Tom Boyd's family is a red tractor family. Steve Boyd's family is a green tractor family.) And pulling still helps keep the clan together, as it has for so many others. It brings them all to the same place, and gives them something to do with their hands while they talk.

Both the Boyds and the Mastersons are Hoosiers, though not exactly neighbors. The Mastersons farm about 3,000 acres down by the Ohio River near Grandview, and the Boyd farms are near Washington, Indiana. Don Masterson, Kevin's dad, bought a John Deere 6030 in 1974. For four years it worked the farm. Then they stripped off the cab, called it *River Rat*, and took it pulling. Seven years later they bought a John Deere 4255 and called it *Tinker Toy*, "because Dad was always tinkering with it," Kevin told *Full Pull Magazine* in 2000.

That tractor won at NFMS in 1987 and 1989. With Kevin driving, the Mastersons won again at Louisville in 1997 and took fourth in the NTPA Grand National points chase. The next year, in 1998, Don

took the honors at Louisville as the 10,200-pound Pro Stock Tractor Finals Grand Champion in *Tinker Toy*.

That same year, Steve Boyd finished in the top 10 in the ATPA points battle, and then rolled into Louisville the next winter and won the 1999 CTP, driving a 10,200-pound Prostock tractor. It was his first try. He went on to win the ATPA Grand American points title in 1999 on *Green Streak*, and took the Bowling Green Ring with *Green Streak II*.

Both families were riding a wave of victories as the 2000 Grand American Pulling Series opened in Hamilton, Ohio. The Mastersons, the Boyds, Scott Teipen (the future ATPA points and Winternationals champion), and others were there to get it started. At the end of the first round, 10 of them had gone the distance for the pull-off.

Of the 10 competitors, Kevin and Don Masterson went one and two, Kevin beating his dad by 3 feet. Right behind them was Steve Boyd's son, Greg, on *Green Streak II*, with Greg's brother Mike farther back on the original *Green Streak*.

The contest was renewed at the Warrick County Fairgrounds— another great pulling venue in Boonville, Indiana, not far from the Boyd farms. The TV cameras were rolling and a big crowd turned out in the scorching, dripping heat to see 21 Prostocks toe the line. Both Mastersons, both Boyds, Bobby Sarver, and Scott Teipen made full pulls,

Don Masterson of Grandview, Indiana, drives his 10,200-pound Prostock tractor. When the Mastersons bought the John Deere 4255 in 1981 they called it "Tinker Toy." Kevin Masterson told *Full Pull Magazine* it earned its name "because dad was always tinkering with it." Much more than a toy, the 10,200-pound Prostock pulling machine won the Louisville Championship Tractor Pull three times—1987, 1989, and 1998. Don Masterson took second place behind his son, Kevin, in the 2000 ATPA Prostock points race. *Don Gillespie*

Steve Boyd comes from one of the great Prostock pulling families. The Boyds of Washington, Indiana, took the 1999 and 2001 Prostock Grand American championship and won at the Louisville Championship Tractor Pull. Steve Boyd is shown here aboard *Green Streak II. Don Gillespie*

along with 3 other Prostock tractors. Twenty-one tractors were whittled down to 9.

The lone IH in the crowd came out strong in the pull-off. *Fuelish Pleasure*, driven by Gary Brinkmeier, spun out 3 feet short of a second full pull. Kevin Masterson in *River Rat* crept up to his mark, just a little bit short at 296 feet, and the Boyds and everyone else fell in behind. Sarver and Don Masterson, in first and second place in the Grand American points standings, ended up in eighth and ninth place, and the race became a free-for-all from that point on.

Kevin Masterson followed up with a win at Henry, Illinois, less than 3 inches ahead of Trent Boyd, whose wife had given birth just a few nights before. And then the Prostockers were off to Evansville. Here, little-known Phil Parish calmly turned down the first test hook, and came back with the winning run on *El Niño*, another victory for the IH fans. Brinkmeier and Trent Boyd followed him, making it a clean red sweep.

Kevin Masterson managed fourth, giving him enough points to take over the lead, as the Prostock show moved to

Tom Lindsey from Duncansville, Pennsylvania, rides up in the cab of *Built for Business*, a diesel-burning Modified Semi truck pulling in the Big Rigs Series. Lindsey is in search of his sixth national championship in the Modified Semi division. His Cummins KT-600-powered, quad-turbocharged Kenworth is the reigning ATPA Big Rigs champion. *Photo Joe Egli*

Goshen, Indiana, where 25,000 fans awaited the next turn of fortune. It was here that the field began to sort itself out.

The Mastersons and Boyds took four of the top five positions in Goshen, and Kevin Masterson started to build a lead on the competition by coming in first by over 11 feet. By the end of the season, the Mastersons were locked in a tight contest for the ATPA points championship with Steve Boyd's two tractors, *Green Streak* and *Green Streak II*, driven by his sons, in third and fourth. By a slim four points, after the final hook, the older generation of Mastersons gave way to the new, as Kevin Masterson notched his first ATPA points championship.

MARTIN AND EDER MODS

As the Boyds and the Mastersons were settling their good-natured Prostock family feud, another pulling family was embarking on a run of NTPA Grand National titles in the Unlimited Modified class.

By then, the various NTPA Modified weight classes had been pared to two—Modified and Unlimited Modified.

Warming up at the 2002 ATPA Winternationals in Fort Wayne, Indiana, is Jeff Hirt and Unlimited Super Stock AGCO *Runnin' Bare*. (Hirt kept the hammer down despite the blaze to the delight of the crowd.) Hirt, winner of the 2001 Louisville Championship Tractor Pull in the 8,000-pound Super Stock Alcohol Tractor division, comes from Port Clinton, Ohio. *Photo Joe Egli*

Jay Fuqua of Springfield, Tennessee, rides in his *Tennacious* 8,200-pound Super Stock Case/IH MX270 at the Louisville Championship Tractor Pull. Fuqua won the event in 2002 in the 8,200-pound Super Stock division driving *Tennessee Tracks*. In 2004 he was back with both tractors, with a new Full Pull Motorsports chassis under *Tennessee Tracks*. The new components helped Fuqua to a sixth-place finish in the 8,200-pound Super Stock class with a pull of 212.45 feet. *Kentucky Fair & Exposition Center*

Mike Savey of Hillsboro, Kentucky, pulls an Ironman sled Saturday, February 15, 2003 at the Louisville Championship Tractor Pull. *Canadian Mist III* is Savey's Super Stock JD 7810. *Kentucky Fair & Exposition Center*

Prostock puller Larry Shope wins the 2002 Grand American season opener on June 3 at the Salem Speedway in Salem, Indiana. Fourteen Prostocks competed in 95-degree heat, including Steve Boyd on *Green Streak*, Lance Little on *Gang Green*, and Bobby Sarver, but the only full pull belonged to Shope on *Iron Dragon*. Shope has won five Grand National Prostock titles since 1998. *Photo Joe Egli*

Darren Smith of Crittenden, Kentucky, sits on 8,200-pound Super Stock *Walking Tall,* at the 2003 Louisville Championship Tractor Pull. At the ATPA Winternationals on January 18, 2003, Smith worked the tractor into a pull-off with Darrell Meese on *Squealer*, Larry Phillips on *Insanity*, and Randy Payne on *Guess Work.* Smith took second place behind Meese. *Kentucky Fair & Exposition Center*

Richard Ziegler of Waunakee, Wisconsin, drives a 7,500-pound Modified tractor named *P-38* because it is powered by twin 1710-ci, 2000-horsepower Allison V-12 engines, just like its namesake P-38 fighter, which fought in World War II—Ziegler's Allisons are stair-stepped, while the old Lockheed fighter engines were side by side. *Kentucky Fair & Exposition Center*

Modified now means a maximum weight of 7,500 pounds, and limitations on the type and number of engines. Unlimited means just that—*unlimited*.

There, among the Unlimited tractors, the Martin brothers from Bonnie, Illinois, staked their banner in 2000. Following Grand National championships in 1998 and 2000 in the Modified class, Tom and Rodney Martin ran off with three straight wins. From 2000 to 2002 they dominated the heavyweight class, before bowing to Gardner Stone and his 12,000-horsepower turbine tractor, *The General Stage IV*, in 2003.

In the lighter Modified class, by 2003, Joe Eder was emerging as an outstanding puller among those whose tractors look like dragsters. It was the year he brought home his second Grand National championship, and the way he did it left fans speculating on the possibility of more to come.

In the first session at Tomah, Eder took 16th place, leaving him 12 points behind Doug Downs' *Predator*, 1999 Grand National Modified champion and his main competition. With *Predator* running well and consistently, Eder could not afford to lose another hook. And he didn't. Eder passed Downs at final pull in Bowling Green for the title.

Ken Measel of Almont, Michigan, drives *Mining for Dollars*, a Case/IH 7250 8,000-pound, alcohol-burning tractor. This picture was taken at the 2003 NFMS Saturday Finals, in which Measel placed third behind Terry Blackbourn and Jordan Lustik. Earlier in the year, Measel was the runner-up to Lustik in the 2003 ATPA Winternationals. *Kentucky Fair & Exposition Center*

Kurt Wileman of Edgerton, Wisconsin, drives *Die Hard Deere*, a 10,200-pound Prostock Tractor. It was a battle of the Wilemans for the 2003 NTPA Region III points championship in the Prostock division. Kurt Wileman beat both Kraig Wileman in *Die Hard 2* and Bob Lemke of Helenville, Wisconsin, in *New Generation Plus* by a single point. The Wilemans pull for K&K Equipment. *Don Gillespie*

Modified 4WD puller R. B. Moler of Harpers Ferry, West Virginia, drives *To The Xtreme.* Moler won the ATPA Lucas Oil Power Middle U.S. Super Region point title in 2003, a scramble that came down to the final pull at the Tennessee Valley Fair in Knoxville, Tennessee, September 5 and 6. With only a slight lead in the points chase, Moler came in 12th on Friday night. Fortunately for Moler, Steve Clem's *Ratical,* his nearest competitor, also fared poorly and came in 10th. On Saturday Moler had the division's only full pull, beating Clem, who came in fourth. When the scores were tallied, Moler won the championship by one point. *Don Gillespie*

Competitor Terry Hagedorn from Thompson, Missouri, drives his 4WD Modified Chevy *Untamed Spirit*. A decade in drag racing helped the Hagedorns, Terry and Sheila, build horsepower and chassis expertise for the tractor pulling circuit, in which they have seen consistent success. In 1995, the couple entered their first Grand National event, and the Hagedorns won first and second place. Terry went on to win the Grand National championship and Rookie of the Year honors. At the 2004 Winternationals finals, *Untamed Spirit* pulled past Gary Varner in *Fast Break* and Steve Clem's *Ratical* for Terry Hagedorn's first Winternationals title. *Don Gillespie*

Lisa Tatum of Bardstown, Kentucky, stands before her Super Modified 2WD Chevrolet-bodied truck *Full Throttle*. In 2003, at the age of 21, Tatum became the first woman to win the Louisville Championship Tractor Pull 6,200-pound 2WD Super Modified Truck division. Pulling is a family affair with the Tatums, as Lisa's father, Tony Tatum, drives the family's second supercharged Chevy-bodied pickup, *Xtreme Pleasure*, and Lisa's brother T. J. is the team crew chief. *Don Gillespie*

Eder's fans are most excited about the scope of his success. He won the Grand National points title and the ATPA points title; at the NFMS in Louisville, he took three straight in the 7,500-pound Modified tractor class, from 2002 to 2004.

At the ATPA Winternationals in 2004, Eder's domination of the Fort Wayne event continued as he scored his sixth win in a row in the multiengine Lucas Oil Super Modified Tractor class. His four blown Chryslers roared to the only full pull mark, easily snuffing a bid by 2003 ATPA title-holder Jerry Stewart out of Paris, Tennessee in *Down 'N Dirty*, at 286.9 feet.

While Eder has made his presence felt throughout the Modified pulling world, the NTPA 2WD division has become the domain of Craig Nation, son of L. D. Nation. Craig grew up watching his father compete in first the Super Stock and later the 2WD division. "I've seen a lot of stuff go down the track, since I was a year old," he said in a 2003 interview in *The Puller*. After watching his dad take four Grand National titles (two in 1989, one each in 1991 and 1992) and his brother, Brent, win in 1990, it was Craig's turn in 2000, 2002, and 2003. With eight Grand Nationals between them, it might seem like winning holds no challenge to Craig and the Nation team, but the thrill of victory is still alive.

"What makes it exciting is when you win," he said. "You beat the best, so that's the way you want it."

Dominating the ATPA's side of the track in the 2WD truck division in 2003 was Stan Shelton, of New London, North

Carolina, and his *Cutting Edge* Ford. Besides winning the ATPA points title, Shelton won the 2WD truck Winternationals in 2004. In the Winternational finals on January 17, 2004, Shelton showed real strength, wheel-standing down the track 306 feet for the winning pull. Roger Simon of Farley, Iowa, in his Dodge, *Simon Sez*, claimed second at 296 feet.

BIG RIGS AND SUPER SEMIS

In the NTPA Super Semi division, since the turn of the century, Greg Hibbitts and *Pro-Hibbitted* have been nearly unstoppable. The *Pro-Hibbitted* team is currently riding a string of Grand National championships that run back to 2001.

The truck is a beautiful blue Kenworth with a Caterpillar 893 diesel engine, and the driver is a successful businessman from Hudsonville, Michigan. And with Gary Rairigh and

Lance Little of Tuscola, Illinois, driving *Gang Green,* a John Deere 5020 smoker. Little won the Prostock Shootout at the 2002 ATPA Winternationals in Ft. Wayne, Indiana. *Don Gillespie*

Al Hopkins in the shop taking care of the 20,000-pound semi truck, there were no major breakdowns in the 2003 pulling season, leading to Hibbitts' third straight victory.

Under the ATPA banner, 2003 was another great year for the Lindsey family from Duncansville, Pennsylvania, as Tom Lindsey drove home the Lucas Oil Big Rigs title in *Built for Business*.

The Lindseys, who own both ATPA and NTPA semi truck championships, are one of the few husband and wife pulling families in which both spouses drive. In 2002, Tom's wife, Dana Lindsey, won the ATPA Big Rigs title in *Red, Hot and Rollin'*, a big red Peterbilt with a Cummins KT-600 inline six with three turbos. Tom was second. That was only payback from two years earlier, when Tom won the championship and

With this able crew, the Super Stock tractor *Silver Bullet* won the 2004 NFMS Championship Tractor Pull. It was the team's second straight win at Louisville, and third overall. On Thursday night, February 12, 2004, in the 8,000-pound Super Stock Alcohol Tractor division, *Silver Bullet* beat Joe Kwiatkowski in *Taking Care of Business* and Larry Roberts II on *The Big Toy* in a three-way pull-off. In the Saturday night finals, *Silver Bullet* faced another pull-off, this time with Roberts' teammate John Evans in *The Big Toy II*. The big White AGCO won by five feet. *Don Gillespie*

Carl Smith of Greenfield, Indiana, won the ATPA Prostock championship in 1999, in *Night Moves*, shown in this photo. The pair teamed up for a second ATPA Grand American title in 2002 on the strength of five event wins, with four in a row scored early in the season. Smith also had three second place finishes and a couple of thirds. His total was 45 and 69 points ahead of two-time and ATPA world champion Steve Boyd's *Green Streak* and *Green Streak II*. Smith also has a Championship Ring victory at the National Tractor Pulling Championships in Bowling Green, Ohio. *Don Gillespie*

This engine shot is from the hood of *Spellbound*, Tom Tormoehlen's 6,200-pound 4 x 4 Modified truck. Always a tough competitor on the pulling circuit, Tormoehlen of Vallonia, Indiana, won the ATPA Grand American 4 x 4 truck championship in 2002 with 572 points, beating Steve Clem's *Ratical* with 557, and 2001 ATPA Grand American champ Jim Bosch with 551. *Don Gillespie*

Dana took second. It was the first time in major pulling history when a husband and wife team went one and two for a title.

THE TRACK AHEAD

These races have only whetted the appetite of pulling fans for the 2004 season. So many questions will be answered by midsummer. Can Jordan Lustik add another ATPA Unlimited Super Stock title? Can Greg Hibbitts make it four Grand Nationals in a row?

With NTPA excitement building in places like Tomah, Wisconsin, and Bowling Green, Ohio, and ATPA action being prepared for Henry, Illinois, and Macon, Missouri, only this is certain—there will be dirt in the air, big tires on the ground, and friends and family in the stands. And this summer, like the last, tractor pulling will bring us to the track.

With everything the last 50 years of pulling has brought us, the best is yet to come.

The backdraft from this four-wheeler raises a cloud of dust at this ATPA Championship series event from the summer of 2003. Driving the Chevy *Backdraft* is Bill Kear of Knoxville, Tennessee. *Don Gillespie*

Index

2WD division, 58, 75

2WD Super Modified
  Truck division, 57, 88

2WD Truck division, 89

3 Bears, 64, 70

4 PLAY, 46, 73, 75

4WD class, 53

4WD truck division, 70

Afrons, Art, 51, 52

AGCO-White 6195, 15

Alcohol Tractor division, 65

Allis-Chalmers 220, 22

American Tractor Pullers
  Association (ATPA), 51, 53,
  64, 71, 77, 78

Archer, Dave, 57, 60, 67

Arfons, Art, 24, 25, 30, 31, 53,
  55, 61–64

Arfons, Dusty, 53, 55

ATPA Winternationals, 65, 73, 81,
  83, 84, 87, 89

Backdraft, 93

Bad Dog, 23

Bad Medicine, 65

Bandit, 50, 55, 62

Banter, Ralph and Dave, 20,
  25–29, 37, 40, 41, 44,
  50–52, 55, 59, 60, 62–64

Barga, Ron, 28

Batliner, David, 19

Bend, Bob, 22, 28

Berg, Bill, 40

Big Green Machine, 53

Big Toy, The, 90

Blackbourn, Terry, 68, 69, 84

Blagraves, Stan and Steve, 70

Bockwitz, Johnny, 47

Boland, Bill, 29

Bonner, Richard, 16

Bosch, Jim, 75, 92

Bosse, Carl and Paul, 25

Boyd Steve and Tom, 77–81,
  83, 91

Brabec, Dennis, 33, 48

Brinkmeier, Gary, 80

Brockmann, Jim, 62, 63

Brown, 41, 46

Buck Eater, 74

Buckeye Bulldog, 74

Buck's Fever, 66

Built for Business, 80, 90

Bulls Eye, 94

Cain, Tim, 77

Canadian Mist III, 82

Carey, Larry, 74

Case/IH 7250, 84

Case/IH MX270, 82

Chamberlin, Ralph, 22, 28

Chevy Thunder, 59

Clem, Steve, 86, 87, 92

Collins, J. R., 74

Conner, Bryan and Ernie, 65, 66

Country Girl, 50, 59

Cutting Edge, 12, 72, 73, 89

Dean, Danny, 23, 29, 38

Dickerson, Tom, 59, 66

Die Hard 2, 85

Die Hard Deere, 85

Diesel-only Super
  Stock division, 68

Dirt Slinger, 12, 71

Dirtslinger T, 58

Dodge Fever, 74

Down 'N Dirty, 89

Downs, Doug, 10, 84

Eads, Tadd, 63

Eder, Joe, 10, 13, 59, 60, 64, 71,
  84, 88

El Niño, 80

Engler, Tim, 37, 40, 41, 44, 46,
  52, 56, 60

Enterprise Machine, 53

Evans, John, 90

Fast Break, 87

Freday, Lem, 53

Frock, Bob, 24, 25

Fuelish Pleasure, 80

Full Throttle, 88

Fuqua, Jay, 82

Gang Green, 83

General Stage IV, The, 51, 54, 84

Goodgine, Mike, 57

Goodwin, Dennis, 66

Goodwin, Matt, 59

Green Extreme, 74

Green Gate Savage, 68

Green Monster, 51, 52, 55,
  62, 63

Green Power Special II, 35

Green Streak, 78, 81, 83, 91

Green Streak II, 78, 79, 81, 91

Green, Norm, 34

Guess Work, 83

Hagedorn, Terry, 87

Haley, Dave, 28

Hanslovan, Ed, 53

Harness, Don, 32, 34

Harrison, Noble, 22

Heavy Super Stock class, 29

Heriot, J. R., 22

Hibbitts, Greg, 74, 89, 90, 93

Hileman, John, 41, 43, 53

Hirt, Jeff, 81

Holman, Jim and Paul, 46, 53,
  70, 73, 75

Horst, Dennis, 42, 70

Hubert, Danny, 58

Hutcherson, Bruce, 34, 37, 46

IH 1066, 29

IH 1466, 22, 23

IH 3688, 36

Imposter, 48

Indiana Rascal, 63

Indy Super Pull, 28, 34, 38–40,
  42, 48, 50, 53, 56

Indy Tractor Pull, 27, 59

Insanity, 83

Irish Challenger, 57

Iron Dragon, 70, 83

Jaske, Steve, 52

John Deere 4255, 78

John Deere 4320, 35, 44

John Deere 4430, 70

John Deere 6030, 78

John Deere 7810, 82

John Deere 9200, 17

Johnson, Stan, 47

Jostock, Bob, 13, 59, 64

Kear, Bill, 93

Kleikamp, Randy, 73, 75

Kline Jr., Lawrence, 68

Klug, John, 29, 39, 47

Knipstein, Judy, 59, 60, 63, 64

Knox, Rodalyn, 50, 52, 55, 56,
  59, 64

Kock, Al, 34

Krieger, Butch, 19

Kwiatkowski, Arnie, 66, 68, 69

Kwiatkowski, Joe, 17, 65, 90

Lagod, Jerry, 22, 23

Lawrence, Bill, 67

Lehn, Esdon, 29, 39, 47, 53, 59,
  63, 66, 69, 70

Leischner Shannon, 58

Leischner, Bill, 12, 41, 58, 71

Lemke, Bob, 85

Light Modified class, 37

Linder, John and Mike, 39, 44

Lindsey, Dana, 90

Lindsey, Tim, 80

Lindsey, Tom, 90

Little, Lance, 83

Long, Brian, 94

Long, Keith, 94

Long, Ricky, 94

Lorenz, Jon, 57

Loud Mouth Lime, 32

Louisville Championship Tractor
    Pull, 13, 16, 17, 19, 39, 40,
    47, 53, 56, 58, 59, 61, 63,
    64, 66, 67, 72, 76, 78, 79,
    81–83, 88

Lucas Super Oil Modified
    Tractor class, 89

Lustik, Jordan, 15, 18, 56, 66,
    68, 69, 84, 93

Lustik, Richard, 66

Magnum Force, 66

Makin' Bacon Special, 34

Martin Brothers Motorsports, 62

Martin, Tim and Rodney, 57, 59,
    60, 62, 64, 75, 84

Massey-Ferguson 8160, 19

Masterson, Kevin and Don, 76,
    78, 80, 81

McPherson, Richard, 57

Measel, Ken, 84

Meese, Darrell, 83

Mende, Fred, 22

Mining for Dollars, 84

Mission Impossible, 37, 40,
    41, 46

Missouri Raider, 57

Mitchell, Bob, 34

Modified class, 32, 34, 40, 41,
    46, 52, 55, 64, 84

Modified division, 10, 21, 25

Modified Heavyweight class, 37

Modified Mini division, 70

Modified Semi division, 80

Moler, R. B., 86

Mr. Chevy, 51, 55, 59, 62

Mr. Twister, 71

Nation, Brent, 48

Nation, Craig, 48, 89

Nation, L. D., 48, 49, 74, 89

National Farm Machinery Show,
    17, 53, 56, 61, 65, 66

National Tractor Pullers
    Association (NTPA), 14, 16,
    25, 36, 38, 39, 49, 53, 64,
    58, 77

Nemesis, 42

New Generation, 85

Night Moves, 91

NTPA Super Semi division, 89

Odd Couple, 10

Ohio Gold, 53

Old Yeller, 73, 75

Orange, 41

Orient Express, 67

Outlaw Truck and Tractor Pulling
    Association (OTTPA), 64

P-38, 84

Parish, Phil, 80

Payne, Randy, 83

Petro, Randy, 60, 63, 64, 75

Phillips, Larry, 83

Phillips, Scott, 75

Pioneer, 59

Potter, E. J., 28

Predator, 10, 84

Pro-Hibbitted, 74, 89

Prostock class, 57

Prostock division, 85

Prostock Tractor division, 16

Rairigh, Gary, 89

Ratical, 86, 87, 92

Rattler, The, 57

Rawhide, 47

Red Baron, 29, 39

Red Fox, 42, 70

Red Line Fever, 53, 59, 63

Red, Hot and Rollin', 90

Reed, Ronnie, 37, 38, 42, 50

River Rat, 76, 78, 80

Roberts II, Larry, 90

Rooster, The, 29, 38

Ropp, Warren, 53

Rose, Randy, 59

Runnin' Bare, 81

Russell, Rob, 40, 66

Sarver, Bobby, 78, 80, 83

Sarver, Tim, 74

Sassy Massey, 52, 56

Savey, Mike, 82

Sawmill Express, 72

Shelton, Stan, 12, 72, 73, 89

Shope, Larry, 70, 77, 83

Shorter, Mickey, 74

Silver Bullet, 15, 18, 66, 68, 90

Silver Shields, 23

Simon Sez, 69, 89

Simon, Roger, 69, 89

Slowride, 68

Smith, Carl, 91

Smith, Darren, 83

Smith, Glenn, 38

Smith, Norm, 28

Smith, Scott, 64, 70, 73, 75

Sneaky Snake, 57

Solid Junk, 22

Sonnetag, Dave, 65

Sorrento Express, 71

Spellbound, 92

Squealer, 83

Stangle, Dave, 22

Stewart, Jerry, 89

Stone, Gardner, 30, 50–52, 54,
    55, 84

Sullivan, Dickie, 23, 36

Super Farm Tractors division, 19

Super Modified
    2WD Trucks division, 12

Super Modified class, 12

Super Stock Alcohol division, 17,
    57, 69, 81, 90

Super Stock class, 14, 18, 29,
    36, 40, 47, 48, 57, 59

Super Stock division, 22, 34, 68

Super Stock Open division, 17

Superhick, 19

Taking Care of Business, 17, 90

Tatum, Lisa, 88

Tatum, Tony, 88

Tedder, Scott, 71

Teipen, Scott, 78

Tennacious, 82

Tennessee Tracks, 82

Thompson, John, 22, 23

Tinker Toy, 78

To the Xtreme, 86

Tom Cat, The, 72

Tormoehlen, Tom, 92

Two-Wheel-Drive division (2WD),
    38, 49

Unforgiven, 16

Unlimited class, 52, 53, 64

Unlimited Dragster
    Tractor division, 67

Unlimited Modified class, 56, 81

Unlimited Modified division, 75

Untamed Spirit, 87

Varner, Gary, 87

Voreis, Bill, 47, 67, 75

Walking Tall, 83

Walsh, Dave, 55, 57

War Eagle, 36

Wheeler, Bud, 28

Wild Child, 13, 59

Wild Thing, 65, 66

Wileman, Kraig, 85

Wileman, Kurt, 85

Williams, Eugene, 66

Willy Makit, 94

Wolff, Larry, 19

Wolffgang's Warrior, 19

Xtreme Pleasure, 88

Ziegler, Richard, 84

American State Fair
ISBN 0-7603-1917-0

**International
Harvester Tractors**
ISBN 0-7603-1924-3

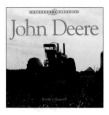

**John Deere: The Classic
American Tractor**
ISBN 0-7603-1365-2

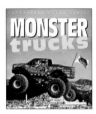

Monster Trucks
ISBN 0-7603-1544-2

**The Illustrated Directory
of Tractors**
ISBN 0-7603-1342-3

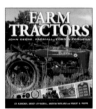

Farm Tractors
ISBN 0-7603-1776-3

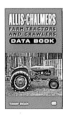

**Allis-Chalmers Farm Tractors
& Crawlers Data Book**
ISBN 0-7603-0770-9

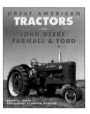

**Great American
Farm Tractors: John Deere,
Farmall and Ford**
ISBN 0-7603-1540-X

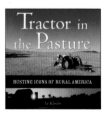

Tractor in the Pasture
ISBN 0-7603-0876-4